BUDDHA

OSAMU TEZUKA

3: *Devadatta*

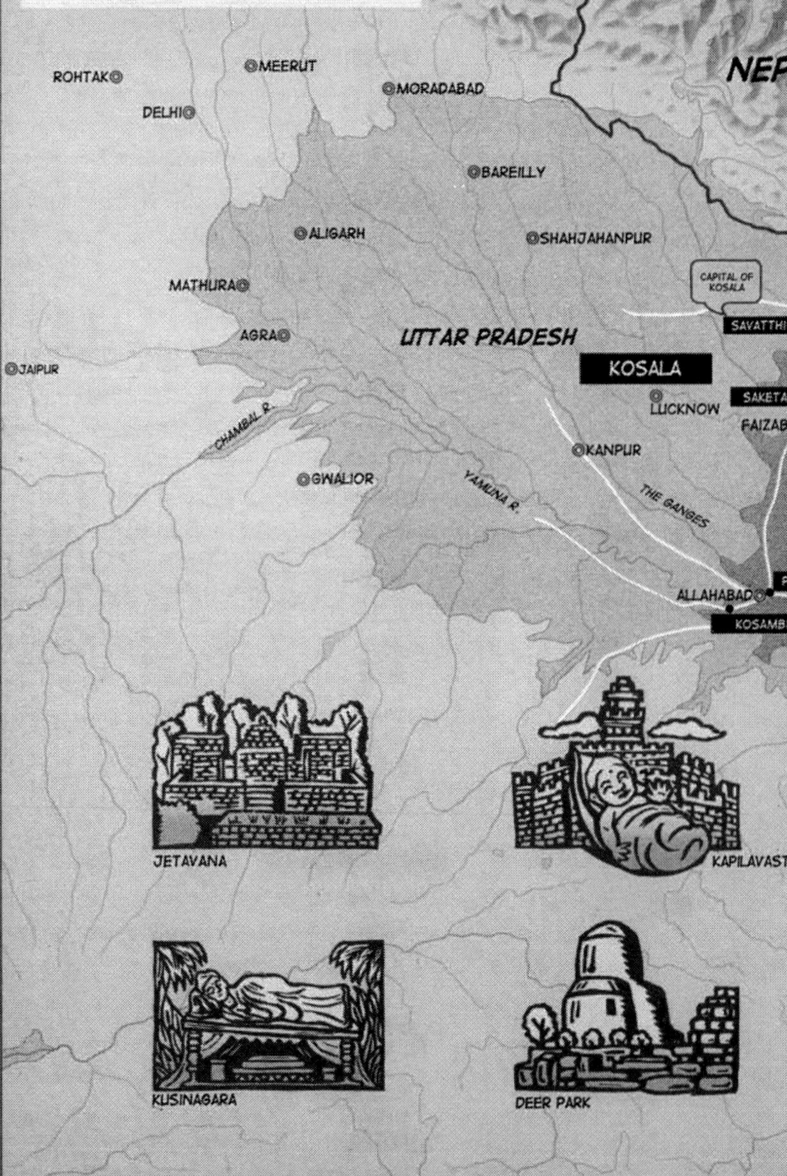
THE JOURNEY
ROHTAK
MEERUT
MORADABAD
DELHI
NEPA
BAREILLY
ALIGARH
SHAHJAHANPUR
CAPITAL OF KOSALA
MATHURA
SAVATTHI
AGRA
UTTAR PRADESH
JAIPUR
KOSALA
SAKETA
LUCKNOW
FAIZABAD
CHAMBAL R.
KANPUR
GWALIOR
YAMUNA R.
THE GANGES
PRA
ALLAHABAD
KOSAMBI
JETAVANA
KAPILAVASTU
KUSINAGARA
DEER PARK
LUMBINI ANCIENT PLACE NAMES
MAJOR ROUTES
PLACES VISITED BY THE BUDDHA

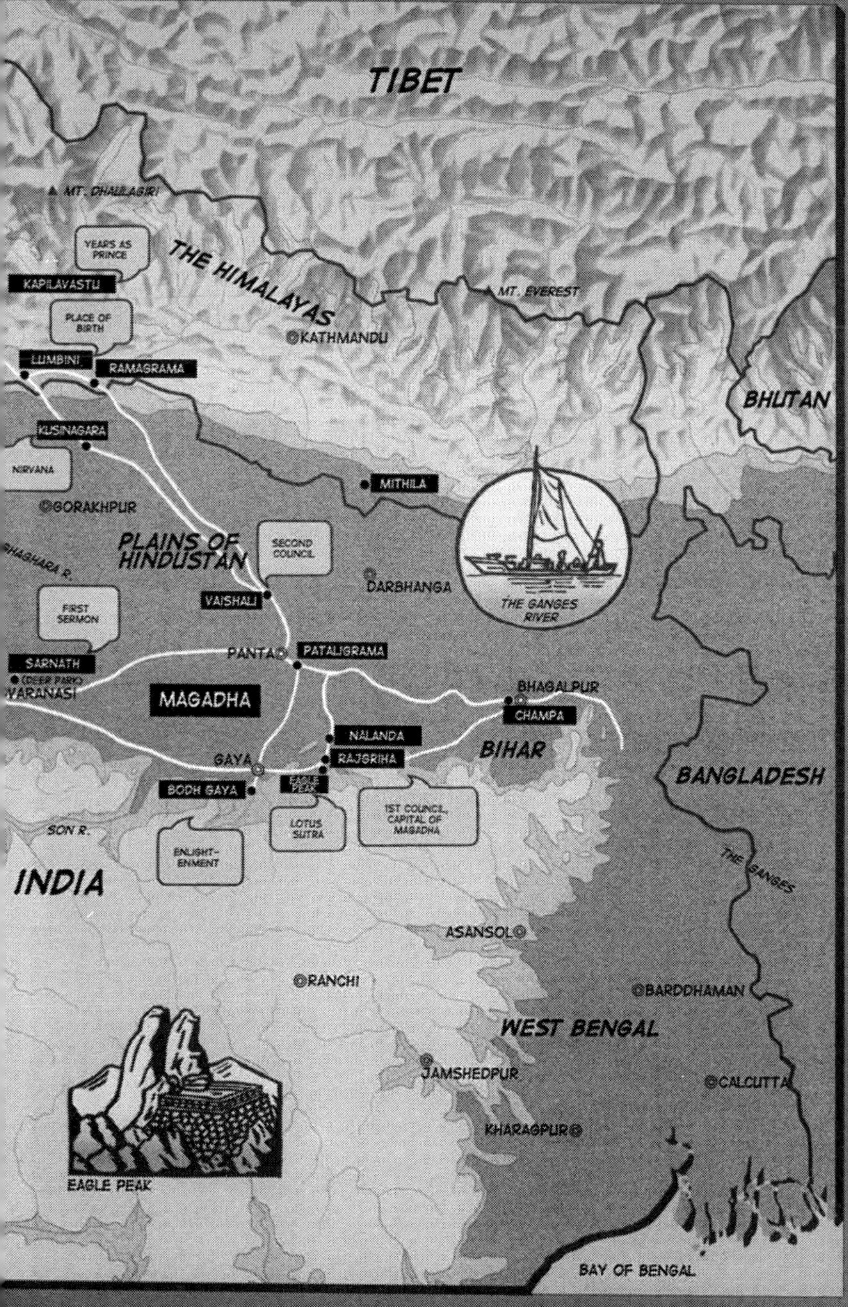

TIBET
MT. DHAULAGIRI
YEARS AS PRINCE
THE HIMALAYAS
KAPILAVASTU
MT. EVEREST
PLACE OF BIRTH
KATHMANDU
LUMBINI
RAMAGRAMA
BHUTAN
KUSINAGARA
NIRVANA
MITHILA
GORAKHPUR
PLAINS OF HINDUSTAN
SECOND COUNCIL
GHAGHARA R.
DARBHANGA
VAISHALI
FIRST SERMON
THE GANGES RIVER
PANTA
PATALIGRAMA
SARNATH
(DEER PARK)
VARANASI
BHAGALPUR
MAGADHA
CHAMPA
NALANDA
BIHAR
GAYA
RAJGRIHA
BANGLADESH
BODH GAYA
EAGLE PEAK
1ST COUNCIL, CAPITAL OF MAGADHA
SON R.
LOTUS SUTRA
ENLIGHT-ENMENT
INDIA
THE GANGES
ASANSOL
RANCHI
BARDDHAMAN
WEST BENGAL
JAMSHEDPUR
CALCUTTA
KHARAGPUR
EAGLE PEAK
BAY OF BENGAL

HarperCollins*Publishers*
77–85 Fulham Palace Road,
Hammersmith, London W6 8JB

www.harpercollins.co.uk

Published by HarperCollins*Publishers* 2006

A catalogue record for this book
is available from the British Library

ISBN-13 978-0-00-722453-1

The artwork of the original has been produced as a mirror image
in order to conform with English language.
This work of fiction contains characters and episodes
that are not part of the historical record.

Printed and bound in Great Britain by
Clays Limited, St Ives PLC

CONTENTS

PART THREE

PART THREE

CHAPTER ONE

THE ORDEALS

TWEET CHIRP
TWEET CHIRP

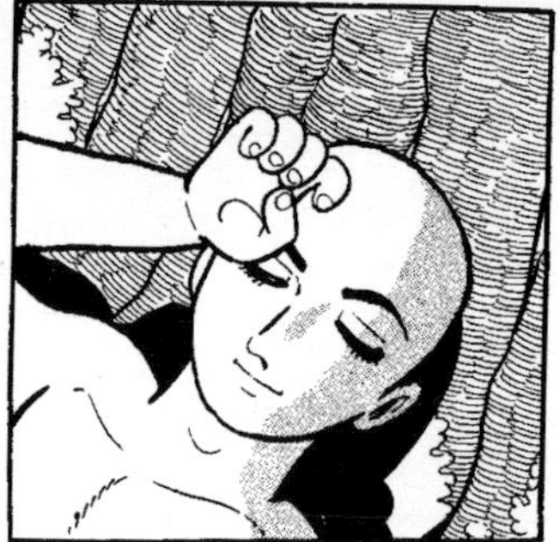

WHAT A GLORIOUS DAY...

THE MOST SPLENDID ONE I'VE WOKEN TO IN MY LIFE.

GOOD MORNING TO ALL OF YOU!

O SUN! MAY YOU ILLUMINATE MY WAY! GREAT SKY, LEAD ME TO THE ENDS OF THE EARTH! CLOUDS! WINDS! LAVISH YOUR TRIALS UPON ME! LIFE AND ALL THAT LIVES, CONSECRATE MY JOURNEY!

FORGIVE ME, COULD YOU SPARE SOME CLOTHES?
MIGHT'VE SAID "HELLO" FIRST...
AH, NOW, DIDN'T SEE YOU'RE JUST A KID. NEWLY SHAVED, TOO.
READY FOR ORDEALS, EH ?
YES, I'M HEADED FOR MAGADHA.
WELL, I'M IMPRESSED, BUT...
I BET THE GOING'S TOUGH FOR A YOUNG MONK LIKE YOU.
LISTEN, THIS OTHER MONK HAPPENS TO BE STAYING WITH US.
WHY NOT TRAVEL WITH HIM? HE MIGHT GIVE YOU HEART.
IT'S SETTLED! WE HAVEN'T GOT MUCH, BUT YOU'LL COME SUP WITH US.

CHECK IT OUT, MISSUS! I FOUND ANOTHER ONE!
WELL, I'LL BE DARNED! THAT'S SOME LUCKY STREAK WITH THE MONKS, EH?
AH, BUT LOOK AT HIM, HE'S BARELY EVEN A NOVICE. PIPING HOT AND FRESH FROM THE OVEN.
OH, BUT HE'S SO C-U-U-TE!
AND SO GRACIOUS TOO... THIS BOY'S FROM A GOOD FAMILY, I BET.
HE'S IN THAT SHED,
THE OTHER MONK...
HONEY... ... HISS...
YUP. DON'T NEED YOU TO PROD ME.

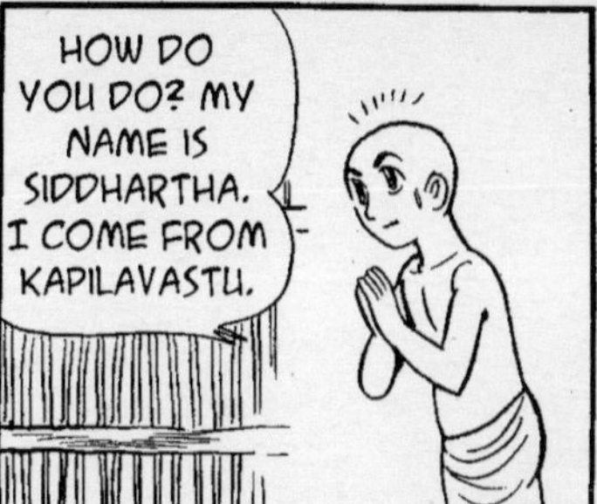
HOW DO YOU DO? MY NAME IS SIDDHARTHA. I COME FROM KAPILAVASTU.

I'M DHEPA, OF KOSALA. REGARDS.

I BECAME A MONK JUST YESTERDAY.
HAVE I HEARD YOUR NAME BEFORE?
AH, YES. YOU'RE NAMED AFTER YOUR COUNTRY'S PRINCE. HA HA HA

WILL YOU TEACH ME? I DON'T KNOW ANYTHING YET.
CERTAINLY, WHATEVER I CAN.

COME AND GET IT!

SO LITTLE? AND WHAT'S TO GO WITH IT?
SHUSH! WE MONKS NEED NO MORE!

IF YOU SAY SO.

GRIK
ECH ECH

PICK UP EVERYTHING YOU JUST SPAT OUT AND EAT IT AGAIN.
EACH AND EVERY GRAIN!
BUT THIS RICE IS FULL OF SAND...

HOW DARE YOU SPIT OUT YOUR FOOD!
DON'T YOU KNOW THE MEANING OF A MEAL?

EAT IT, DAMN YOU! IT'S WHAT UNDERGOING TRIALS IS ALL ABOUT.

GRIK

UH, UM... ACTUALLY, I GOT A FAVOR TO ASK...

TRUTH IS, WE GOT, ER, 32 KIDS, AND THE OLDEST, HE WANTS TO BECOME ONE OF YOU SKINHEADS, I MEAN, A MONK...

THE LITTLE SNOT DOESN'T KNOW HIS PLACE!

NO MONK EVER CAME FROM POOR HUNTER STOCK, I TELL HIM.

BUT IN THIS DAY AND AGE WHEN ACTORS RUN FOR OFFICE, I HEAR POOR FOLK CAN TURN MONK.

HE IS MY BRIGHTEST KID, THAT I'LL SAY FOR HIM.
WE WOULD BE GRATEFUL! SO GRATEFUL! HIS NAME IS ASSAJI.
SNIF
GRIN
PHOOT
HE'S TOO YOUNG... AND I DON'T THINK HE'S CUT OUT FOR ORDEALS.
I WON'T TAKE HIM.
WHAT? YOU TELLING ME MY SON'S NOT GOOD ENOUGH?
HONEY, BOLT THE DOOR!
RUN
AND BRING ME SOME ROPE. I'M GOING TO TIE OUR BOY TO THAT MONK IF THAT'S THE ONLY WAY!

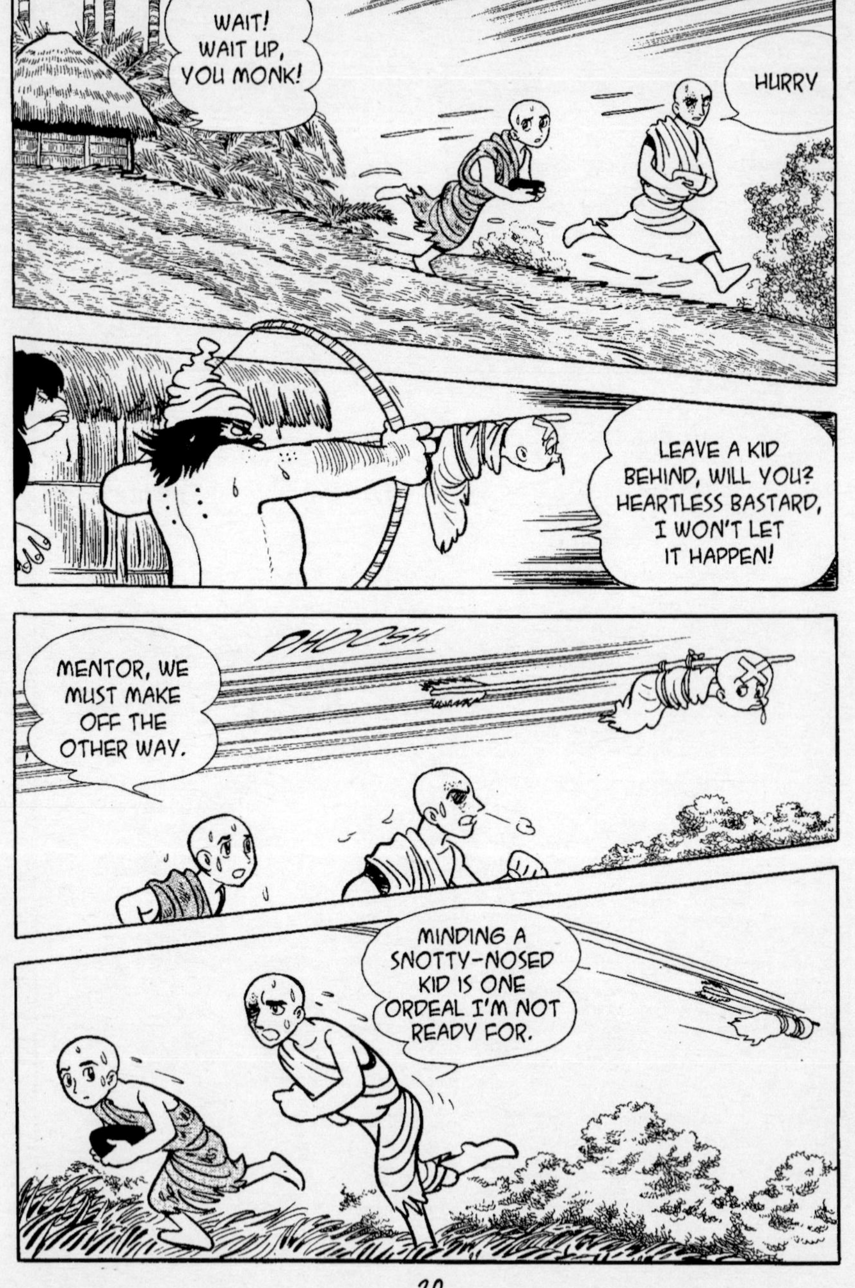
HURRY
WAIT! WAIT UP, YOU MONK!
LEAVE A KID BEHIND, WILL YOU? HEARTLESS BASTARD, I WON'T LET IT HAPPEN!
PHOOSH
MENTOR, WE MUST MAKE OFF THE OTHER WAY.
MINDING A SNOTTY-NOSED KID IS ONE ORDEAL I'M NOT READY FOR.

IF I MAY BE SO RUDE...
MAY I ASK ABOUT YOUR EYE?
AH, THIS? I BURNED IT OUT MYSELF.
YOU DID?
YOUR OWN EYE?
THAT'S RIGHT, IN A DEN OF THIEVES. THEY WANTED TO WITNESS AN ORDEAL.
SO I BURNED OUT MY EYE.
YOU ARE DERANGED.
...

TAPAS (ORDEAL) ALSO MEANS "HEAT."

IT USED TO MEAN EXPOSING YOURSELF TO THE HEAT.

YOU'D SIT UNDER THE BLAZING SUN AND BUILD BONFIRES ON ALL FOUR SIDES. "THE FIVE HEATS," THE TORMENT IS CALLED.

BUT, MENTOR...
DON'T THESE ORDEALS WRECK ONE'S BODY?

AH, YOU DON'T LOOK TOO STRONG.

I'M NOT.
I WAS BORN WEAK...

HMM, IF THAT'S TRUE, YOU WON'T BE ABLE TO ENDURE ORDEALS.

IN THE GREATEST ORDEAL I EVER SAW...

A MAN HAD LOWERED HIMSELF FROM MAN TO BEAST.

I SPEAK OF MY MASTER NARADATTA. HE CRAWLED ON ALL FOURS, NEVER SPEAKING, BLIND IN BOTH EYES. HE ATE INSECTS AND MAGGOTS, AND WAS NOT ABOVE EATING FECES. COULD ANY ORDEAL BE HARSHER THAN HIS?

BUT THAT'S JUST UNREASONABLE. WHY BE SO EXTREME?
NOT FOR THE ORDEAL ITSELF, BUT TO FIND THE COURAGE TO PERSEVERE.
LOOK OVER THERE.
A FIELD OF THORNS. IF YOU WALK THROUGH IT, YOU WILL BE COVERED WITH CUTS FROM HEAD TO TOE.
ARE YOU READY?
...
...

DHEPA, WAIT! PLEASE!
DON'T GO...
OUCH!
OW OW OW OW

PLEASE DON'T LEAVE ME BEHIND.
DHEPA!!
COME ON, YOU CAN MAKE IT.
OW... DAMN IT, DOESN'T HURT, DOESN'T HURT!
COOL, WET GRASS. COOL, WET...

BATHE AND CLEANSE YOUR WOUNDS.

NO. IT'LL STING.
DO YOU WANT YOUR WOUNDS TO FESTER? STOP BEING A FOOL.

...
...

ACH... ICK UGH ECH OH-OH
OUCH HELP!

SIDDHARTHA, THAT TRIAL WAS HARDLY EVEN A PREAMBLE.
THERE IS AN ORDEAL WHERE YOU DEPRIVE YOURSELF OF AIR...
SMART
STING

WHEN YOU STOP BREATHING, FIRST THERE IS RINGING IN YOUR EARS. THE RINGING STARTS TO PIERCE YOUR BRAIN. THEN COMES THE PAIN, LIKE THE LASHES OF A WHIP UPON YOUR HEAD.
YOUR BREATH, WITH NOWHERE TO GO, DIVES INTO YOUR ABDOMEN. IT FEELS AS THOUGH YOU ARE BEING GUTTED ALIVE.

TO WIT...

DHEPA?
ARE YOU OKAY?

...

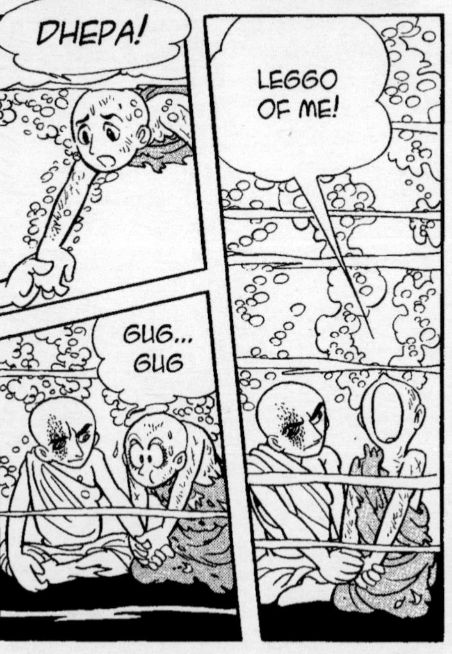
DHEPA!
LEGGO OF ME!
GUG... GUG

LET GO! NOW!! I... CAN'T... BREATHE!
I'LL DIE, I'M DYING!!

HOAAAHH!

I'VE HAD ENOUGH.
WHAT'S THE USE OF SUFFERING LIKE THAT?

YOU BETTER GET USED TO IT. SPIRITUAL PRACTICE BEGINS WITH ORDEALS...
...AND ENDS WITH ORDEALS!
THAT'S STUPID! WHY IN THE WORLD SHOULD WE SUFFER AND SUFFER AND SUFFER?

SIDDHARTHA, SHUT UP NOW AND GET BACK IN THE WATER.

NO, I DON'T THINK –
HM?

PLOSH

WE'LL SWIM TO THE FAR SHORE.
SNIF

AH... LOOK! WE'RE COMING TO VAJJI.

IN THAT COUNTRY LIVES AN ASCETIC NAMED BHAGAVA. I'M QUITE ANXIOUS TO MEET HIM...

IN HERE? WHAT KIND OF ORDEAL IS HE ENDURING IN HERE?
HE IS HAVING VULTURES PICK AT HIS FLESH.

WHAT DID YOU SAY?!
INSIDE, THE PLACE IS FULL OF VULTURES. THE HERMIT LIES IN THEIR MIDST.

HEY! WHO SAID YOU MAY GO IN?
AH!!
Flap
Flap
GAW
THIS IS TERRIBLE!!

THESE BONES ARE HIM?
WHAT GOOD DID IT DO HIM IF IT ENDED UP KILLING HIM?
THIS IS WHAT YOU GET FOR ALL YOUR SUFFERING?
TELL ME, DHEPA.
NOW YOU SEE WHY I'M SKEPTICAL OF ORDEALS.
YOU HAVEN'T GOT A CLUE, HAVE YOU?
TO DIE IN AN ORDEAL IS PURE GREATNESS! IT IS THE SUPREME IDEAL!
WELL, I DISAGREE. DYING DOESN'T SOLVE A THING. IT CAN'T BE THE ANSWER.
UM
YOU SEE, I DON'T WANT TO DIE.
OR ARE YOU TELLING ME THAT LIFE DOESN'T MATTER?
MAY I REMOVE THE CORPSE?
BUNCH OF FOLKS COMING THIS WAY! COULD BE BRIGANDS!

GOOD MONKS, RUN FOR YOUR LIVES!
rumble
rumble
rumble
rumble

GALLOP
GALLOP
GALLOP
GALLOP
GALLOP

CLOP
CLOP
CLOP

FOUND YOU AT LAST!

REMEMBER ME? A LONG, LONG TIME AGO, WE WENT A-BOATING FROM YOUR KAPILAVASTU ALL THE WAY TO THE BORDER OF MAGADHA. DON'T SAY YOU'VE FORGOTTEN TATTA!
AND HERE'S THE WENCH WHO HAD SUCH A CRUSH ON YOU BACK THEN. MIGAILA'S MY WIFE NOW, AND SHE HAS A GANG OF HER OWN AGAIN!

HOW YOU'VE CHANGED! I DIDN'T RECOGNIZE YOU.
HMM, AND ANOTHER FAMILIAR FACE...

SIDDHARTHA, I'VE COME TO FETCH YOU. YOU'VE NO IDEA HOW HARD I LOOKED FOR YOU.
LET'S GO HOME.
HOME? WHAT FOR?
DON'T BE DIM, EH?
LOOK AT YOU, REALLY GONE AND TURNED MONK. THAT'S ONE SORRY-LOOKING NOGGIN.

YOU GOTTA BECOME THE GREATEST KING ON EARTH AND CONQUER KOSALA; I'M COUNTING ON YA.
SO DROP THAT SHABBY LOOK, GROW SOME HAIR, AND PUT ON THAT CROWN OF YOURS, I SAY.
YES OR NO, MY GREAT SIDDHARTHA?

HERE, EVEN FOUND YOU A WIG.
DON'T BE SHY, MEN'S WIGS ARE ALL THE RAGE THESE DAYS.
I'M GOING TO BECOME AN ASCETIC. PLEASE, DON'T GET IN MY WAY!

HEY, HEY...YOU'VE FORGOTTEN WHAT I TAUGHT YOU WAY BACK WHEN.
YOU'VE GOTTA ENJOY LIFE. LOVE, POWER, MONEY, YOU NAME IT – LIFE CAN GIVE IT TO YOU.
WHY GIVE ALL THAT UP?

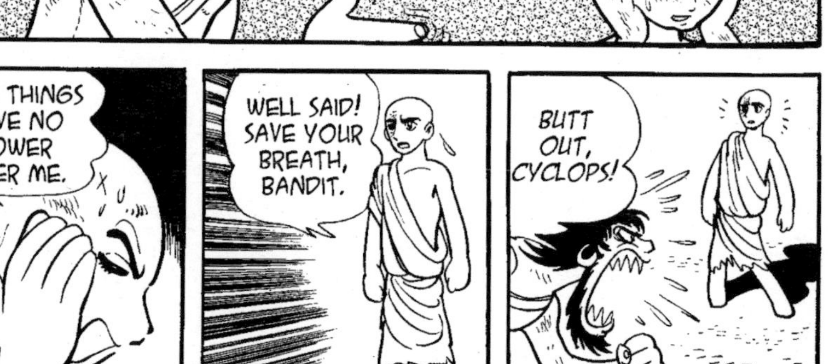
SUCH THINGS HAVE NO POWER OVER ME.
WELL SAID! SAVE YOUR BREATH, BANDIT.
BUTT OUT, CYCLOPS!

WELL, IF YOU'RE REALLY SO FIRM IN YOUR RESOLVE...
I HAVE NO CHOICE. I'M COMING WITH YOU!

I'M GONNA FOLLOW YOU, MAN, WHEREVER YOU GO.
ME TOO!
GIVE ME A BREAK!
LISTEN, FELLERS! WE TWO'LL BE GOING OFF ON A JOURNEY!
YOU'LL BE ON YOUR OWN. HOLD THE FORT AND KEEP IT TIDY.
CAN YOU RIDE?
OF COURSE. I WAS ONCE A WARRIOR. ...NOW!!

SIDDHARTHA!
YOU AREN'T GETTING AWAY, SO DON'T MAKE ME GET ROUGH ON YA!
SHUCKS... ...AFTER HIM, MEN!

CLAP CLAP CLAP CLAP CLAP

gallop
gallop
WELL, I GUESS SIDDHARTHA ISN'T TOO FOND OF US, THE WAY HE SPLIT AND ALL. HEH HEH HEH
DON'T GET HIM WRONG...
I THINK HE'S STILL IN LOVE WITH ME.

I'LL MAKE HIM KICK HIS MONK HABIT FOR GOOD.
I'LL BRING HIM BACK TO THE CASTLE.
AND IF HE KEEPS ON SAYING NO?
HA, THEN I'LL KILL HIM...
WITH MY OWN TWO HANDS!

CLAP
CLAP
HOP
GALLOP
GALLOP
PHEW
HUSH
SNIFFLE
SNIF...

SN
SNF

NOT AGAIN... DUNNO WHY, JUST CAN'T STAND THAT KID.

I WONDER EXACTLY HOW LONG HE PLANS TO FOLLOW US AROUND?

NO IDEA. SOME PEOPLE JUST DON'T KNOW WHEN TO QUIT.

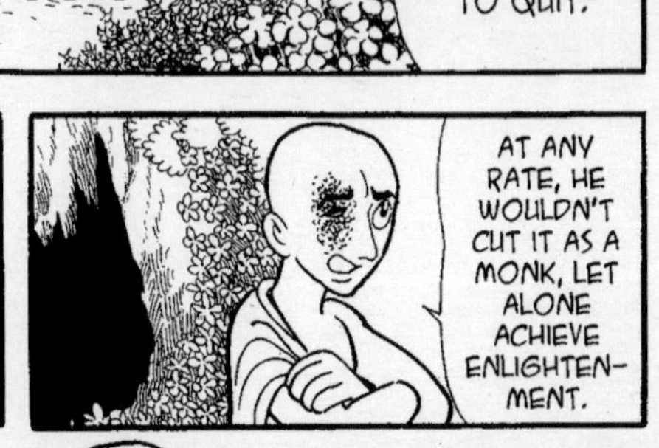

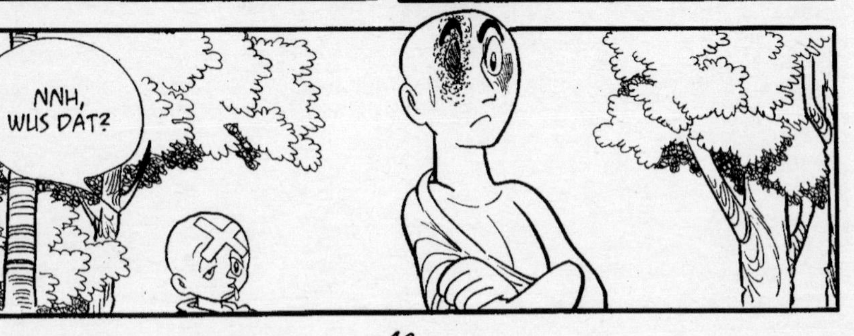

RUN!!

GALLOP
GALLOP
GALLOP
GALLOP

HEY THERE, LAD!!

DID TWO MONKS PASS THIS WAY?
ONE OF THEM ONE-EYED, THE OTHER YOUNG AND LEAN? COME ON, FESS UP, OR YOU'LL BE SORRY YOU DIDN'T.

SIDDHARTHA, WE'RE TRAPPED! THE BRIGANDS ARE BACK!
YEAH, SAW DEM. BUT WUS ID WORTH TA YA?
SNIF

HNH
THIS WAY, MATES!
TROT TROT TROT TROT TROT
YER SAFE NOW.
SO I GUESS YOU'VE SAVED US, AND WE OWE YOU.
YUP
TAKE ME WIT YA?
HMM... I DON'T LIKE THIS AT ALL...
WHAT SHALL WE DO?
LET'S RUN!!
I JUST CAN'T STAND THE IDEA OF HIM TAGGING ALONG!
SNIF

HE'S STILL FOLLOWING US...

HE'S STILL FOLLOWING US! WHAT A STUBBORN KID. WON'T HE EVER LET GO?

SO DID ASSAJI, THE ODD COMPANION, FOLLOW SIDDHARTHA AND DHEPA. THEIR ORDEAL-LADEN JOURNEY IN SEARCH OF ENLIGHTENMENT CONTINUES. BUT WE MUST NOW INTERRUPT OUR STORY SO YOU MAY HEAR OF A FATEFUL CHILD. DEVADATTA IS HIS NAME.

CHAPTER TWO

SURVIVAL OF THE FITTEST

LET US LEAP FORWARD NOW, LIKE A SPRITE ON THE WINDS OF TIME, TO SEVERAL YEARS HENCE. IN A HOUSE ON THE EDGE OF THE TOWN OF KAPILAVASTU, WE SEE A YOUNG BOY, WEAK AND FAINT OF HEART. HE IS DEVADATTA, BORN OF THE WOMAN BANDAKA HAD TAKEN AS QUEEN.

THERE, THERE, MY LI'L ONE.
YUMMY? YUMMY?

THERE YOU ARE, PEEPING AGAIN! DAMN YOU, DEVADATTA!

Thwack
SORRY
Thunk
BEATING THAT BOY AGAIN...
STOP IT!!
Thunk
BE FAIR TO HIM, EVEN IF HE'S ONLY A STEPCHILD TO YOU.
THE KID STARES WITH SUCH ENVY WHEN I FEED MILK TO ANANDA!
ARGH! EVERY TIME I LOOK AT HIM, I SEE HIS BRUTE OF A FATHER, BANDAKA. IT CAN GET ON MY NERVES.
ESPECIALLY WHEN MY REAL SON ANANDA IS SO SWEET!
CAN HARDLY BELIEVE THEY'RE BROTHERS.

YES, I BORE THEM BOTH, AND I LOVE THEM BOTH!!

COME, COME, MY POOR DEVADATTA.

...
...

YOU'RE GOING ON A PICNIC WITH SOME FRIENDS, AREN'T YOU?
YOUR LUNCH IS ALL READY.

THEY PICK ON ME! I DON'T WANNA GO!

YOU JUST THINK SO BECAUSE YOU'RE SO SHY, DEAR.

LOOK, THAT'S DEVADATTA. SPITTING IMAGE OF HIS FATHER, ISN'T HE?
...YOU MEAN HIS REAL FATHER, THAT BANDAKA!
HE'S GOT THE SAME EVIL EYES!

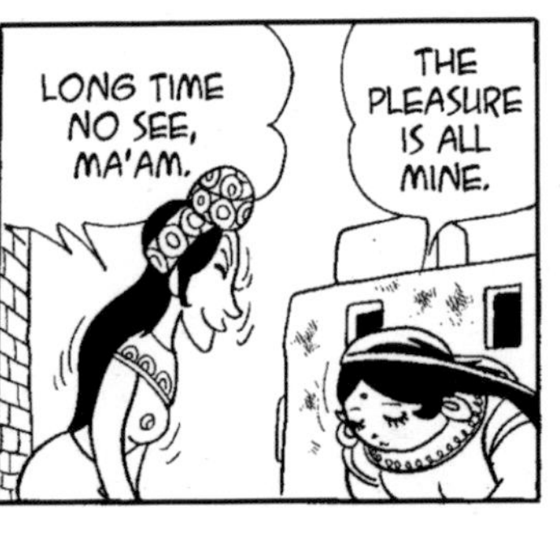
LONG TIME NO SEE, MA'AM.
THE PLEASURE IS ALL MINE.

HEY! THAT'S MY APPLE!
SO WHAT, SQUIRT? YOU ONLY NEED HALF.

THERE'S YOUR HALF.

DON'T COME HOME LATE, OKAY, DEVADATTA?
I'M A LITTLE WORRIED ABOUT SENDING THEM OUT ALONE.
THEY SAY IF YOU LOVE THEM, LET THEM GO.

SO FAR THERE HASN'T BEEN A SINGLE ACCIDENT, I HEAR.
AT LEAST, WHEN THERE'S A BUNCH OF THEM, YOUNG KIDS CAN BE MUCH TOUGHER THAN WE'D CARE TO ADMIT.
I'D FEEL BETTER IF A SLAVE WENT ALONG, BUT THEN THEY'D NEVER LEARN INDEPENDENCE.

BYE MOMMY!

NA-NA!

THE PIGEON COOED
THE PIGEON COOED
A WHITE PIGEON
THE PARAKEET SANG
THE PARAKEET SANG
A RED PARAKEET

YAY YAY
WHEE
HURRAH

CARRY THIS FOR ME, DEVA-DATTA!

MINE TOO.

REALLY? GEE, THANKS.

DEVADATTA, GO GET SOME WATER.
NO
HE'S GOT SOME NERVE!
BUT HASN'T GOT A DAD!
AND YOUR FAMILY'S POOR! MY MOM SAID SO!

HEY, LOOK!
WHINE
WHINE

OOPS, RAN AWAY.
YELP

YOUR DUMB FOOTSTEPS SCARED HIM OFF!

GO FIND HIM!
YEAH! GO CATCH HIM.

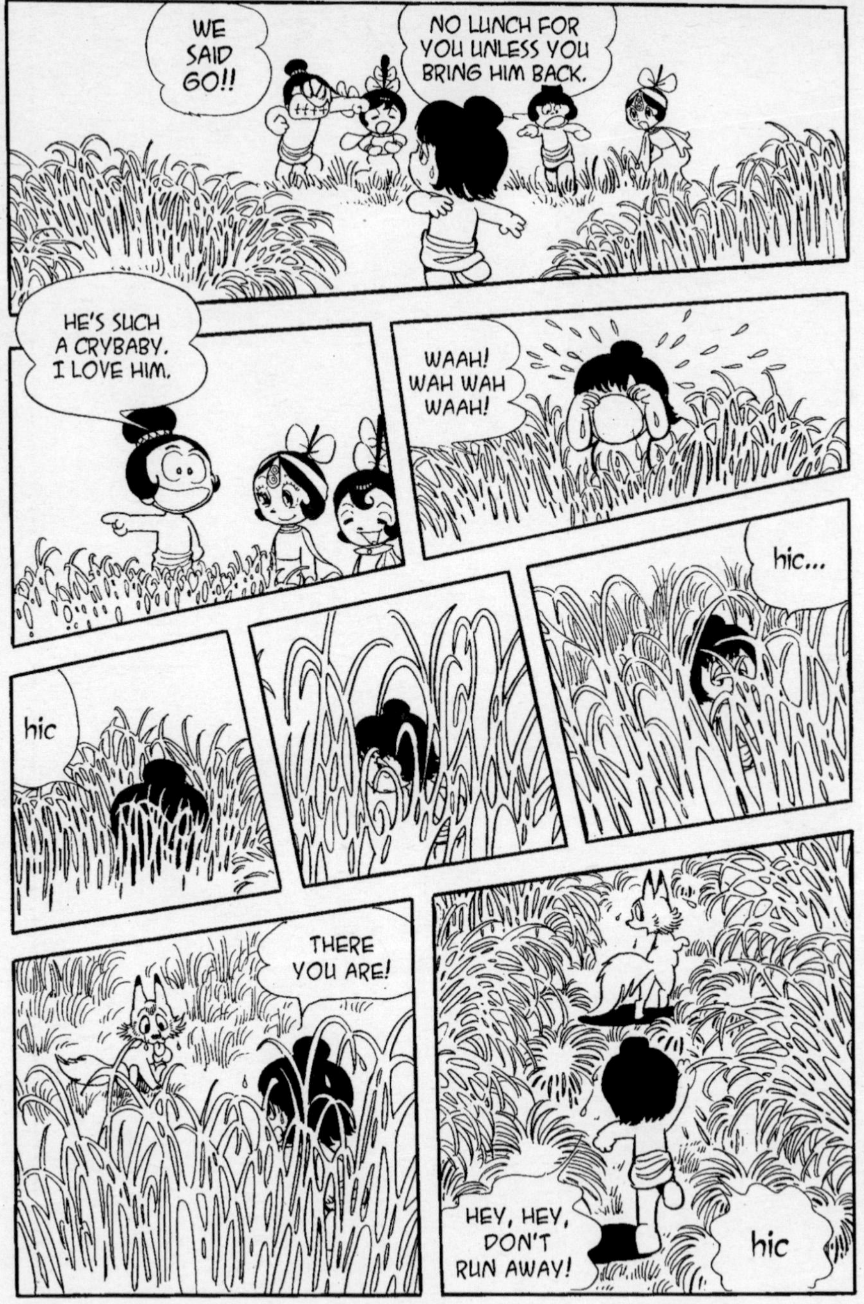
WE SAID GO!!
NO LUNCH FOR YOU UNLESS YOU BRING HIM BACK.
HE'S SUCH A CRYBABY. I LOVE HIM.
WAAH! WAH WAH WAAH!
hic
hic...
THERE YOU ARE!
HEY, HEY, DON'T RUN AWAY!
hic

WAAH

HOWL HOWL

WAIT!

A GIANT SNAKE? ...NO, AN ELEPHANT!

BHOOF!!

HELP!

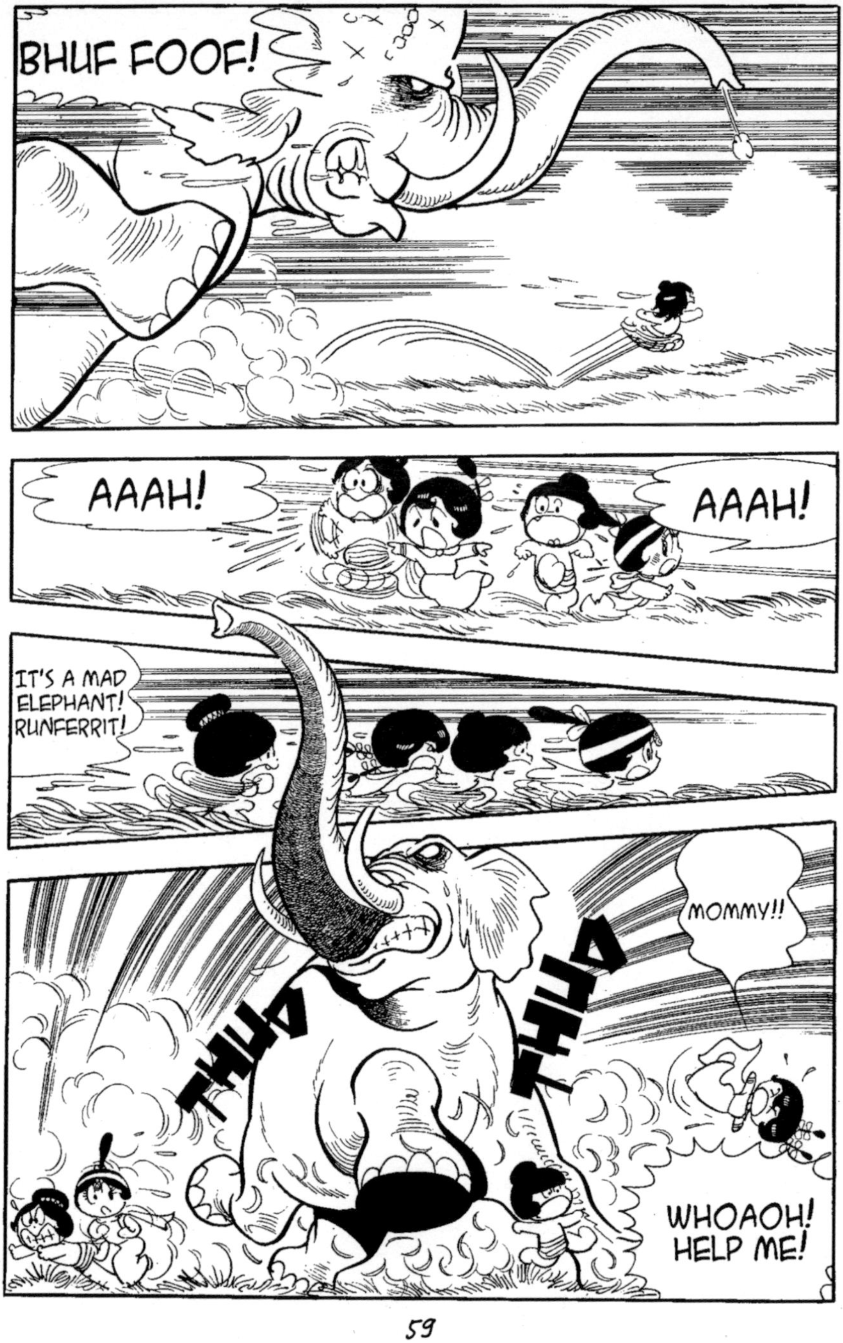

AAAH!

AAAH!

IT'S A MAD ELEPHANT! RUNFERRIT!

MOMMY!!

THUD

THUD

WHOAOH! HELP ME!

PWOOOOF
THUD
PLEASE! I'M SCARED!
THRASH
THRASH
THE HOLE! HIDE IN THIS HOLE!
THUMP
THUMP

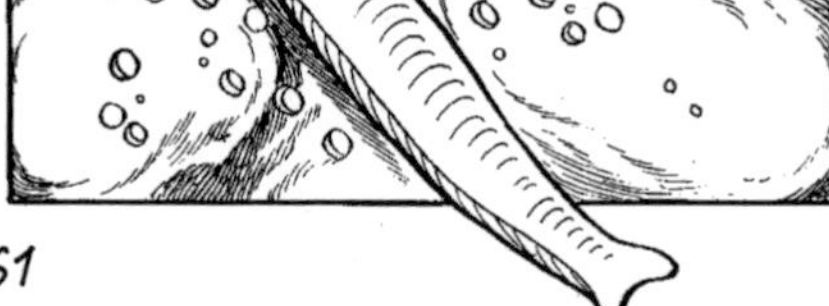
AHHH

QUASH
QUISH

SNORT!!
SNORT!!

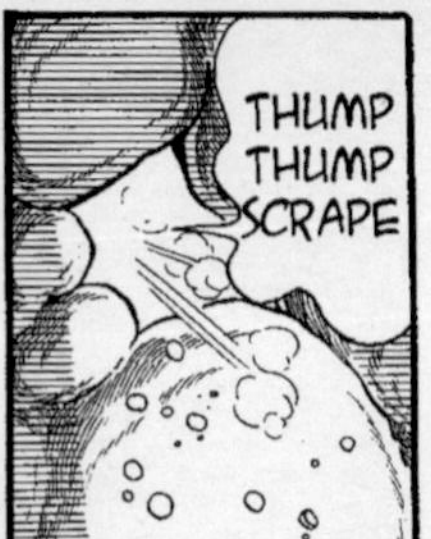

CALM

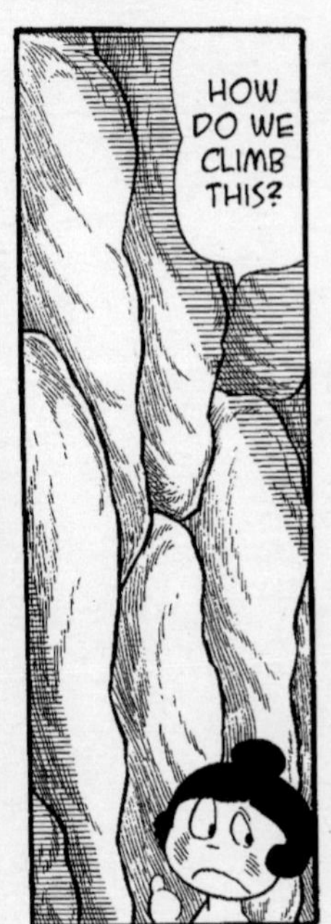

WHY DON'T YOU GIVE IT A TRY, DEVA-DATTA?

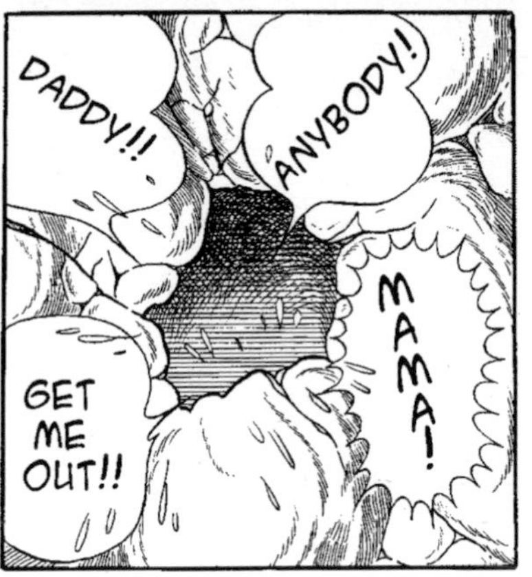
DADDY!!
ANYBODY!
MAMA!
GET ME OUT!!

NIT WIT
ROLL

SOB SOB SOB
WAAH WAH WAH WEEP
GUHH

I'M HUNGRY!

WEEP
WAAH WAH
WAH

I CAN'T BELIEVE HOW THIRSTY I AM.
ME TOO, I FEEL LIKE I'M DYING.
H-H-HEY! THAT'S WATER DRIPPING OVER THERE!
YOU CAN'T!
I FOUND IT FIRST.
IT'S MINE. IT'S ONLY FOR ME!

HOW CAN YOU NOT GIVE US SOME, STUPID!
NUH-UH.

BEAT IT, STINGY. IT'S NOT JUST YOURS, ANYWAY.

CRACK

LIMP
...
IT'S MINE! STAY AWAY, OR I'LL DO THAT TO YOU TOO!

BALA!!
NAGINA!

WHERE ARE YOU ALL?!
CAN'T YOU HEAR US?

ELEPHANT COULDN'T HAVE GOTTEN ALL FIVE. IT'S JUST HARD TO BELIEVE.
EVEN IF THE KIDS DIDN'T ALL GET AWAY, THERE HAVE TO BE SURVIVORS.
THEN FIND THEM! IS MY CHILD ALIVE, OR NOT?
DON'T TALK LIKE THAT!

PANT *PANT* *PANT*
COME ON, GIVE US SOME! PLEEEASE!

LET'S TRY TO CATCH HIM OFF GUARD.
PANT
PANT

PUH-LEEASE? DEVADATTA, WE'RE FRIENDS, RIGHT? ME AND YOU?
PANT

GOTCHA!

GULP...
...GULP...

MASH
SHRIEK

MURDER !!
STOP!

2 WEEKS THEY'VE BEEN MISSING NOW.
2 FULL WEEKS. A LONG TIME TO GO WITHOUT FOOD AND WATER. TOO LONG...
PERHAPS THEY WOUND UP IN ANOTHER VILLAGE AND WERE TAKEN INTO CUSTODY.

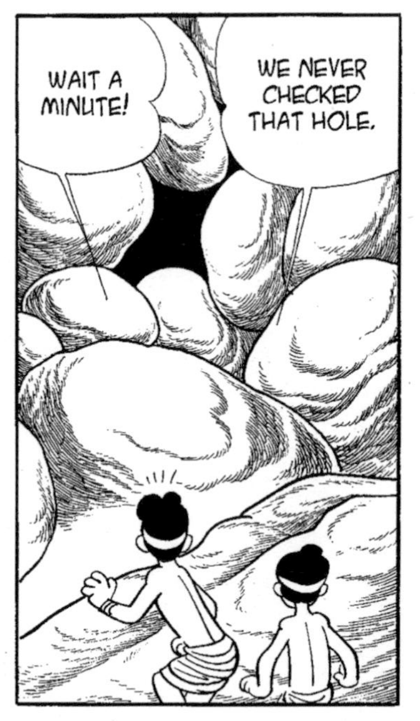
WAIT A MINUTE!
WE NEVER CHECKED THAT HOLE.

HULLO? ANYBODY THERE?

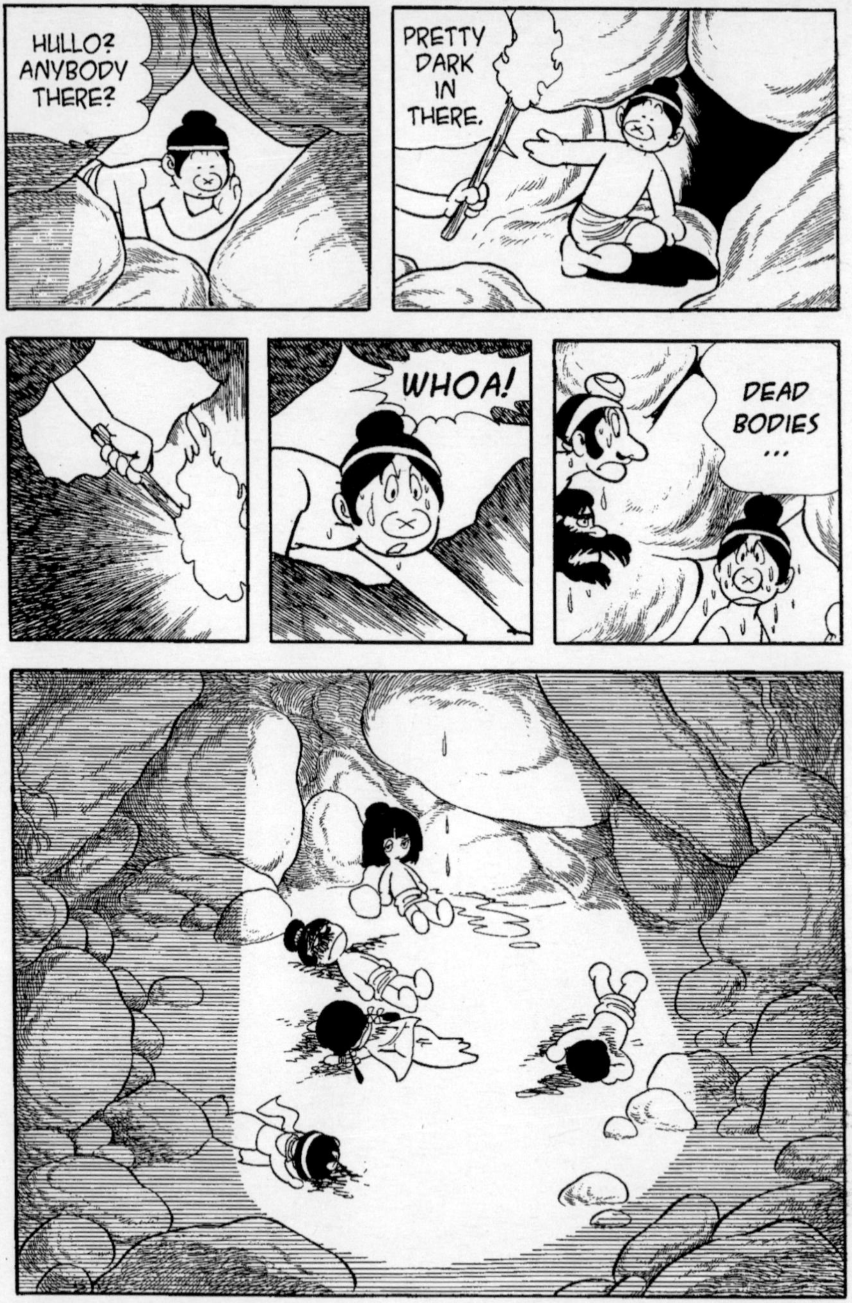

PRETTY DARK IN THERE.

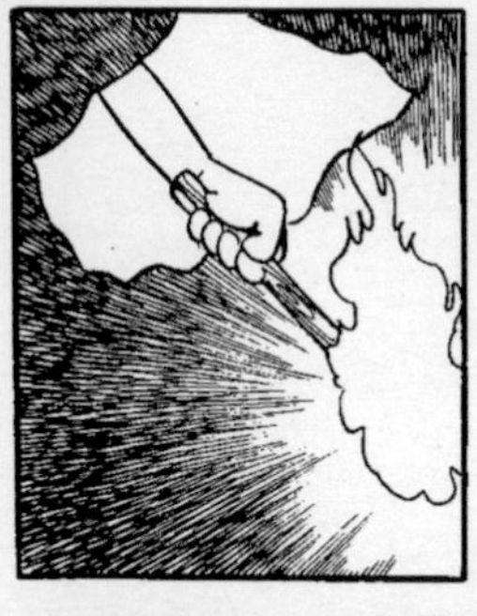

WHOA!

DEAD BODIES ...

SO YOU'RE ADMITTING THAT YOU KILLED THE OTHER FOUR IN ORDER TO SAVE YOURSELF.
MURDERER
BEAST!!
GIVE ME BACK MY CHILD!
NOW, TELL US WHY YOU DID SUCH A TERRIBLE THING.
IT'S MY WATER.
HEH
IF I DON'T WANT MY WATER TO BE STOLEN, THAT'S WHAT I'VE GOT TO DO.

DEVADATTA. WHAT YOU DID WAS AKIN TO THE WAYS OF A HYENA OR A WOLF.
TO STEAL PREY, A HYENA WILL BITE EVEN ITS OWN KIND. NO DOUBT, YOU ARE POSSESSED BY A DEVIL.
DO YOU CONCEDE THAT?

I... YOU'VE LOST ME.

DEVADATTA, TELL HIM IT'S NOT TRUE! BEG FOR MERCY!!

KILL HIM!!
TORTURE HIM TO DEATH!

THERE CAN BE NO MERCY FOR ONE POSSESSED, YOUNG THOUGH HE MAY BE.
WILD BEASTS SHALL BE YOUR EXECUTIONER. YOU SHALL DIE, TORN TO PIECES BY HYENAS AND TIGERS.

THIS WAY, PAL.
DEVADATTA! GIVE YOUR MOTHER ONE LAST HUG!

NOT PERMITTED.
OH... MERCY ...

DEVADATTA!

SCATTERED BONES ARE WHAT YOU'LL BE BY MORNING.
DIE SOON, DEVIL.

MOMMY

MOMMY !!!
I WANNA GO HOME!

GRR... GRR...

GR GRRRL...

SNARL

GROWL

GR?!

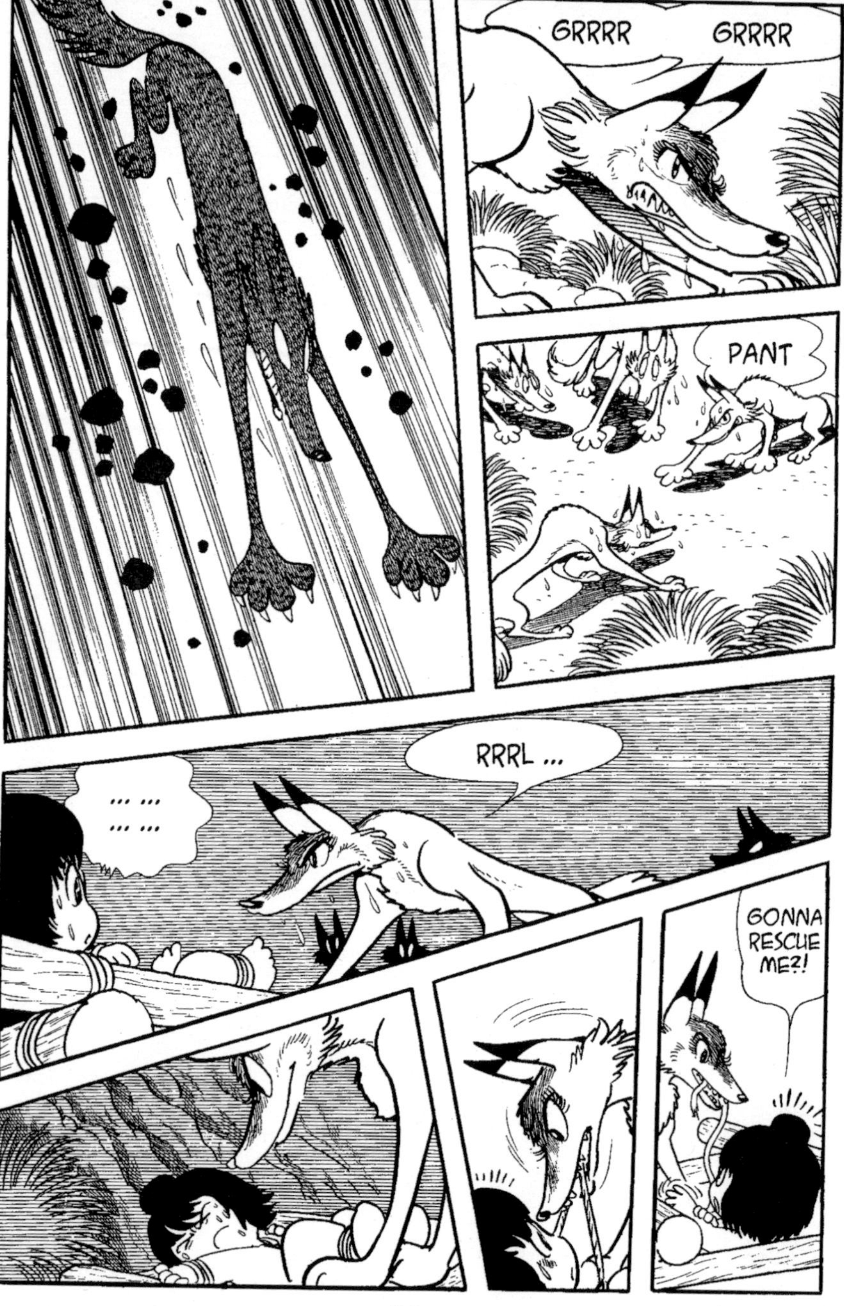
GRRRR
GRRRR
PANT
RRRL ...
... ...
... ...
GONNA RESCUE ME?!

WOOF
GRR... GNASH?
CHOMP?
GEEYOW!
WF WF

HAH HAH
HAAH
HAAH

I REMEMBER
YOU! I
PULLED A
THORN OUT
OF YOUR
PAW.

HAAH
HAAH

PLUMP

?

SUCK
SUCK

MOMMY...
...
I WANNA GO HOME...

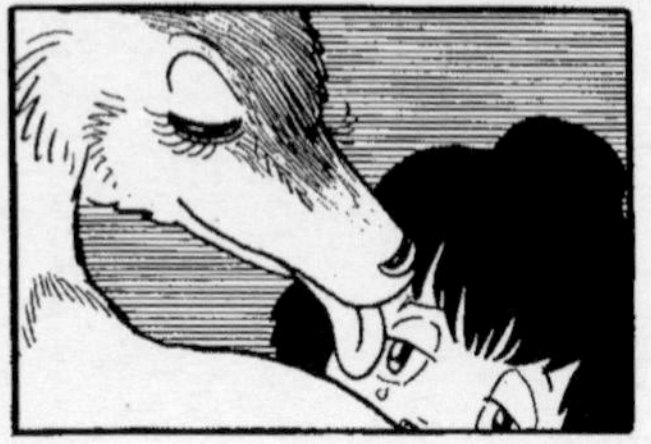

THAT'S MOMMY!
MOMMY !!
OH DEAR, DEVADATTA!
MOMMYYY
WHAT? DEVADATTA IS BACK?
THE DEVIL! HAD THE GALL TO SURVIVE...
HEAR, THE DEVIL IS BACK!
POISON YOUR ARROWS. REGULAR ARROWS WON'T DO THE JOB.

OOPS
WHOOOSH
WHOOOSH
DEVA DATTA !!
MOMMY
WHIFF
WHIFF
I BEG YOU!! PLEASE DON'T KILL MY BOY!!
WHISH
WHOOSH

#CRY#
WUF?

SOB

DEVADATTA CEASED THEN AND THERE TO SPEAK THE TONGUE OF MEN. HE THOROUGHLY DESPISED HUMANS AND TRIED TO FORGET HE WAS ONE OF THEIR KIND.
INSTEAD HE CAME TO LOVE THE MOTHER WOLF MORE THAN HIS BIRTH MOTHER. IT IS SAID THAT CHILDREN RAISED BY TIGERS, WOLVES, AND OTHER WILD ANIMALS HAVE CROPPED UP TIME AND AGAIN IN INDIA. PERHAPS THE REGION'S HARSH CLIMATE CREATED A HABITAT WHERE HUMAN AND BEAST COULD NOT AND DID NOT ALWAYS ESCHEW EACH OTHER.

IN TIME, DEVADATTA LEARNED THAT THE LANGUAGE OF WOLVES ISN'T MADE UP JUST OF GROWLS, BUT ALSO OF GESTURES AND GLANCES.

HEY, BROTHER, LET'S SEE WHO CAN CHASE OUT THE BIGGEST PREY BETWEEN HERE AND THAT HILL.
ME, I DON'T SMELL HUMANS.

...GET SET... GO!
RUSTLE
RUSTLE

FOUND ONE!
!
THIS ONE'S BIGGER
!!
THIS ONE!!
BSSH!

YOU STINKIN' ASSHOLE!

SPLAT
HEY, HERE'S MINE!
WHERE'S YOURS?
...
YOU DID NOT!
UM... I DID.
SCREAM
WAAAH WAA WAAH

MA, FORGIVE ME !! FORGIVE...
I'M SORRY!!
YOU WEREN'T GOING TO EAT IT.
SO WHY DID YOU KILL IT?
BECAUSE YOU'RE A HUMAN.
NOW GET OUT OF HERE!
YER STILL ONE OF THEM!
MA... I WON'T DO IT AGAIN.
I LOST CONTROL ...
YOU CAN'T LIVE WITH US.
WE OF THE WILD KILL ONLY WHEN WE'RE HUNGRY AND WE MUST.
THAT IS OUR LAW!

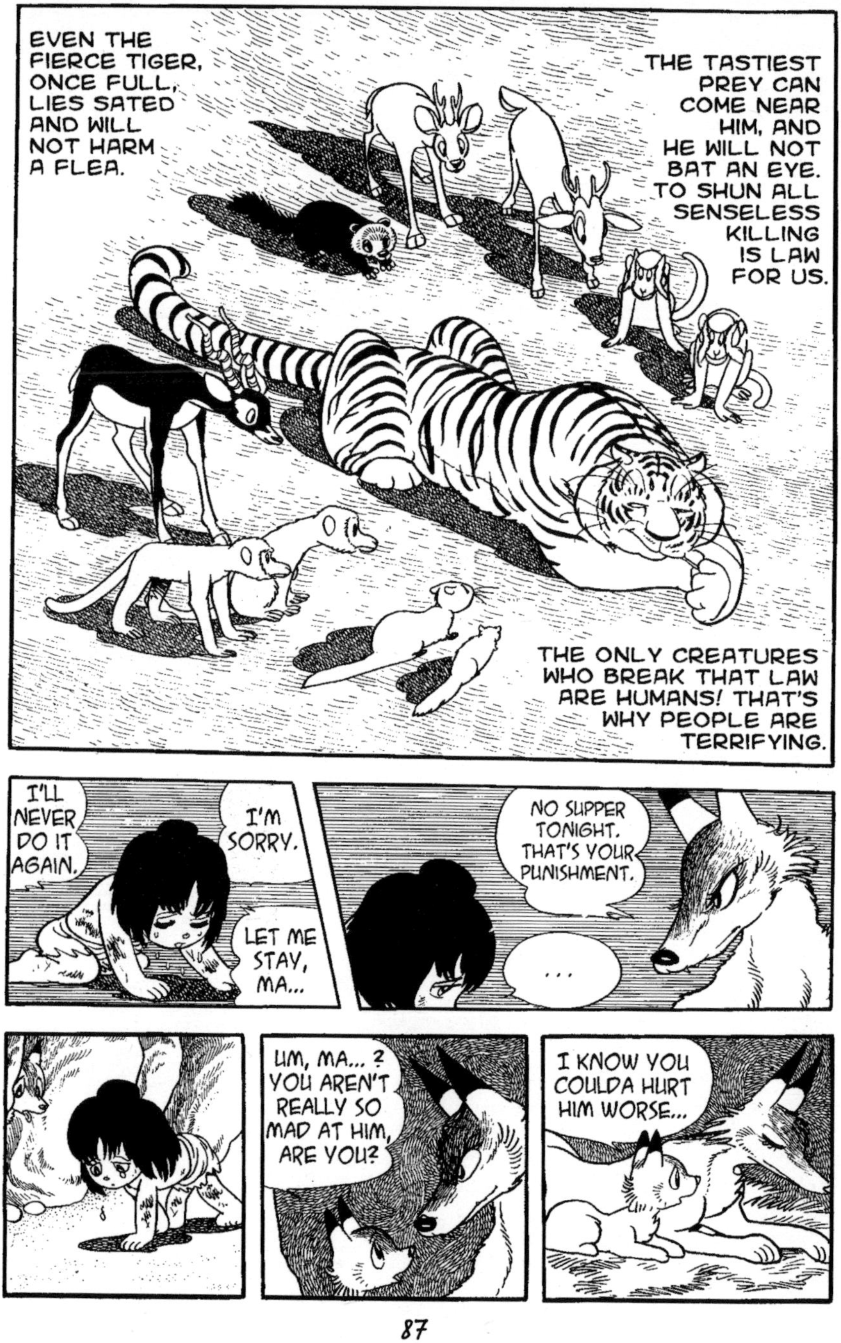

EVEN THE FIERCE TIGER, ONCE FULL, LIES SATED AND WILL NOT HARM A FLEA.

THE TASTIEST PREY CAN COME NEAR HIM, AND HE WILL NOT BAT AN EYE. TO SHUN ALL SENSELESS KILLING IS LAW FOR US.

THE ONLY CREATURES WHO BREAK THAT LAW ARE HUMANS! THAT'S WHY PEOPLE ARE TERRIFYING.

THE DRY SEASON CAME SUDDENLY THAT YEAR, AND IT WAS UNUSUALLY SEVERE. THE HIGH SUN SCORCHED VAST TRACTS OF LAND FOR WEEKS AND WEEKS.

EVERY LAST RIVER EVAPORATED OUT OF SIGHT.

DRY AS A MUMMY WENT THE TREES.

THE ANIMALS PRESSED NORTH, EVER NORTH, SEARCHING FOR WATER. THEY SEEMED TO KNOW BY INSTINCT OF THE GREAT HIMALAYAS' SNOWDRIFTS.

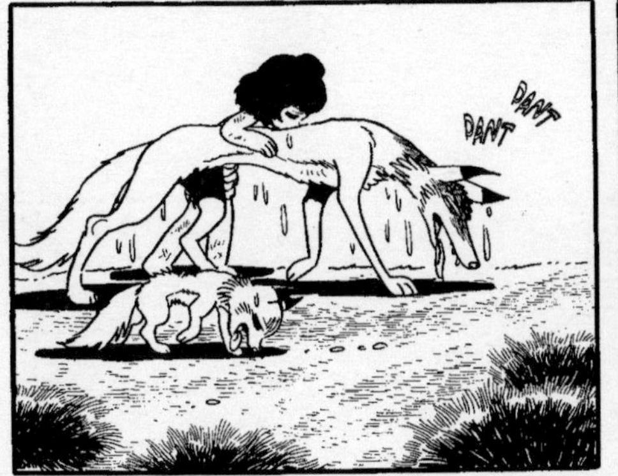
DANT
DANT

GET UP, CHILDREN ...

YOU MUST LEAVE ME, AND GO. IF WE TRAVEL ON TOGETHER, I'LL SOON FIND MYSELF FEASTING ON YOU TWO...
MA... I'M NOT LEAVING YOU!

MA !!
YOU CAN'T
DIE!

SNAP

MA?
GET ON
THIS!

HUP...
DON'T
FALL OFF
NOW.

YOU STILL ARE A
HUMAN, AREN'T YOU?
MAKING A THING
LIKE THIS !

I CAN'T GO ON.

SILLY BROTHER! WE'RE ALMOST THERE!
JUST A BIT FARTHER, AND WE'LL BE AT THE FOOT OF THOSE MOUNTAINS.

THEY LOOMED CLOSE, TRUE, BUT SEEMED ONLY TO RECEDE WITH EACH OF HIS TINY FOOT-STEPS.
STILL, HIS ALMOST RAPACIOUS NATURE SPURRED HIM ON.
MA, HAVE YOU NOTICED? THERE'S NOT ONE CARCASS AROUND HERE. WHATEVER MADE IT THIS FAR MUST HAVE LIVED.
HANG IN THERE, MA, I THINK WE'VE MADE IT.
I SENSE WATER, OVER THAT WAY!
IN THAT VALLEY. LET'S GO!

LOOK!! I THINK WE'RE PRETTY CLOSE!
THERE! WATER!
MA, WATER! HURRY!!
MA!

SHE... SHE'S DEAD.
MA... IF YOU'D ONLY HELD ON A LITTLE LONGER...
LOOK OUT! I'M MOVING THIS ROCK.
SPLUSH

GOOD TO BE HERE.
YEAH! NOW WE'VE GOT TO EAT.

LET'S PLAY HUNTING! HEH, I GUESS FOR REAL THIS TIME.
BIGGEST PREY STILL WINS!

BROTHER, LOOK WHAT I -
NO...
BYE BYE
...
BROTHER!!
WHAT'S THE USE?
YOU CAN STILL GET AWAY! BREAK LOOSE!

BRO

WAA
WEEP
WAIL

HOWL
HOWL

HUH
?!

WHY DO YOU HOWL WHEN YOU'RE HUMAN? AND SO MOURNFULLY?

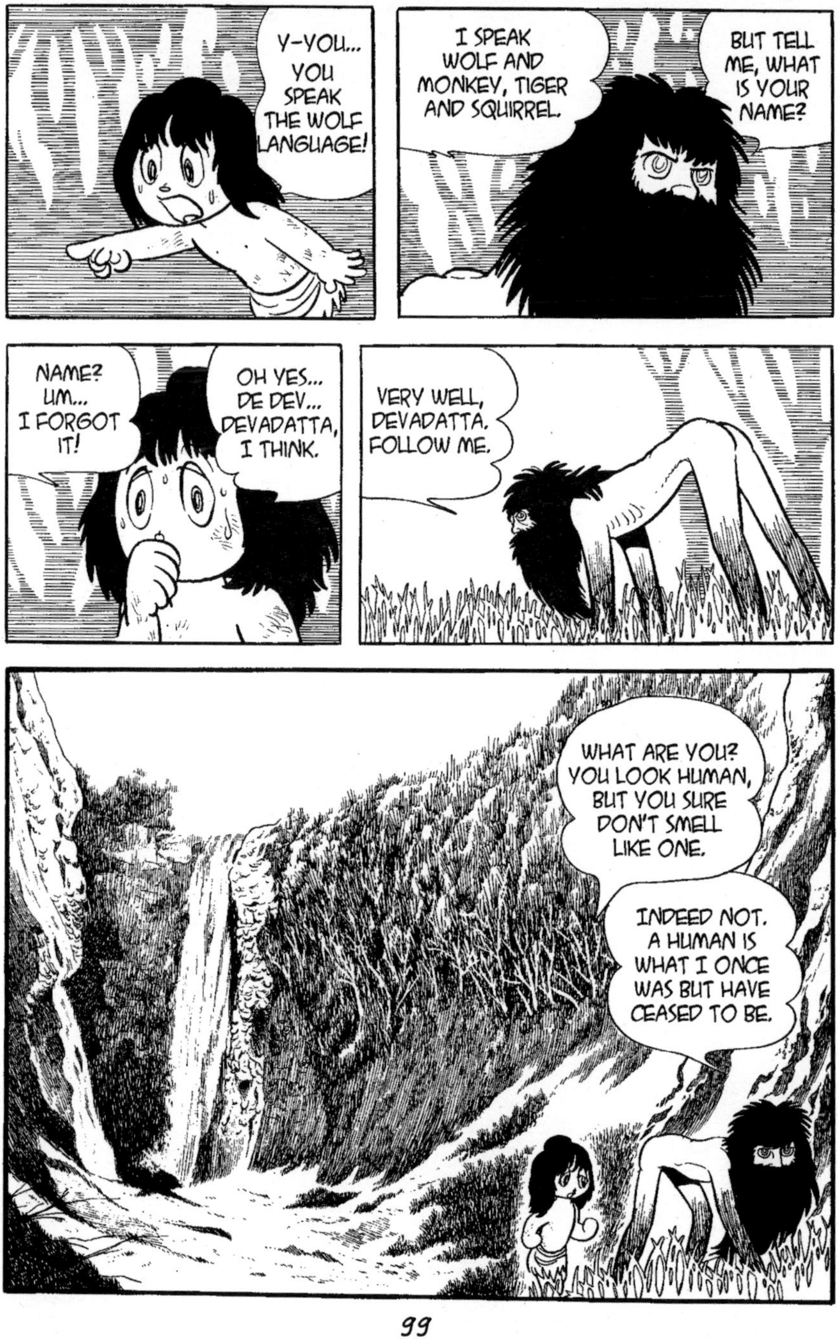

WHAT ARE YOU? YOU LOOK HUMAN, BUT YOU SURE DON'T SMELL LIKE ONE.

INDEED NOT. A HUMAN IS WHAT I ONCE WAS BUT HAVE CEASED TO BE.

DON'T HESITATE TO ENTER. THIS IS MY HOME. THERE IS FOOD, TOO.
REALLY? AND YOU'RE SHARING?

SMELLS WEIRD...

HERE, SOME NUTS. HAVE ALL YOU WANT.

BLEGH
THIS ISN'T FOOD...
WHERE'S MY MEAT?

DIDN'T YOU EAT FRUITS AND GREENS WHEN YOU LIVED WITH HUMANS?

IT'S MORE NOURISHING.
HA! DO I LOOK LIKE A SQUIRREL? THINK I EAT MONKEY FOOD?

MAYBE I'LL EAT YOU INSTEAD.

MA TOLD ME IT'S ALL RIGHT TO KILL PREY IF YOU'RE HUNGRY.
BROTHER'S DYING ON ME PROVED IT!
DO AS YOU PLEASE.

ARGH

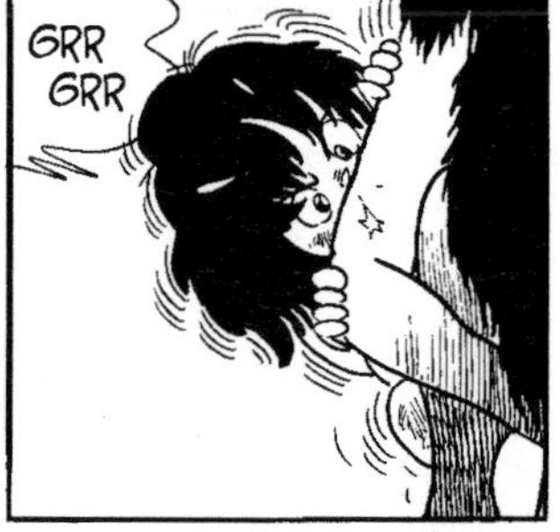
GRR GRR

YOUR TEETH CAN'T TEAR MY FLESH.

SHUCKS!

CHOMP

MUNCH MUNCH

ICK... IT'S ALL WATER!
HASN'T GOT A TASTE.

WOULD YOU RATHER STARVE TO DEATH? IT'LL FILL YOUR STOMACH, AT LEAST.

chew
chew

YOU'RE BLIND, AREN'T YOU.
MY NAME IS NARADATTA. I WON'T ASK HOW YOU CAME TO BE RAISED BY WOLVES. IF YOU WISH TO RETURN TO A PLACE WITH HUMANS, I WILL BE YOUR GUIDE. IF YOU WISH TO STAY HERE AND LIVE WITH ME, YOU MAY.

zzz

SUCH INNO-CENCE.
BRINGS BACK MEMORIES. ...WHAT WAS HIS NAME? YES, TATTA. ABOUT AS YOUNG HE WAS.
SNORE
SNORE

Tweet
Tweet
PICAWWW
PICAWWW

SWASH

RIP
RIP
GNAW
GNAW

Tweet Ti
Tweet Ti
Tweet Ti
Tweet Ti

CHEEP
CHEEP

Chirp

BUZZ

SWAT

NO

BUT HE WAS TRYING TO STING ME!
DO NOT MOVE. BE AS A TREE AND KEEP STILL, OR ELSE YOU WILL BE STUNG TO DEATH.

WHA ?
A TERRIBLE THING IS ABOUT TO HAPPEN. WATCH NOW...

HUMM
AN ENTIRE KINGDOM IS ABOUT TO PERISH. WITNESS A TOTAL MASSACRE.

BUZZ
BUZZ
BUZZ
TWO TRIBES BUILT COLONIES NEXT TO EACH OTHER. THERE WASN'T ENOUGH FOOD TO SUPPORT BOTH.
SMALLER BEES ARE FIGHTING BIGGER BEES!
UNLESS ONE KINGDOM FALLS, BOTH ARE DOOMED. THEY RESORT TO WAR TO DECIDE THEIR FATE.

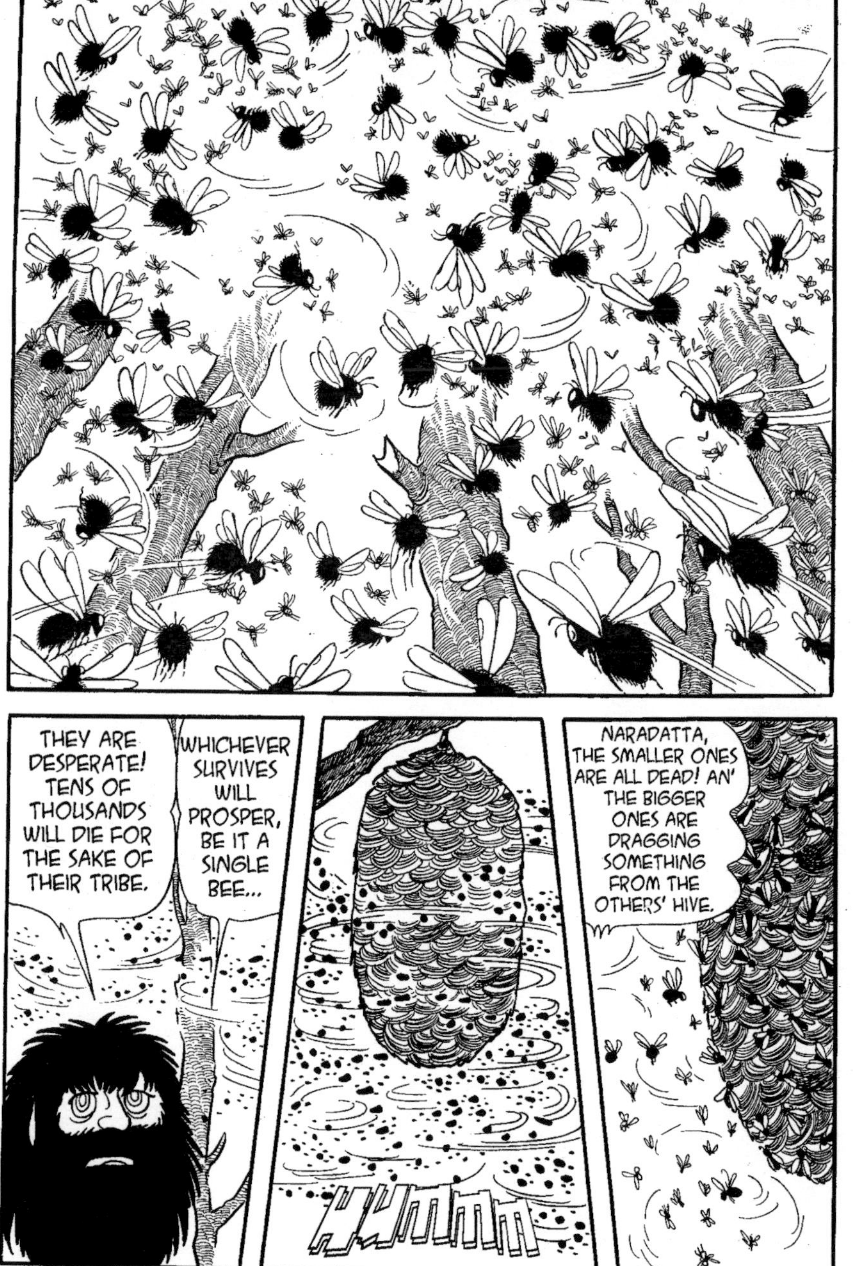

THEY ARE DESPERATE! TENS OF THOUSANDS WILL DIE FOR THE SAKE OF THEIR TRIBE.
WHICHEVER SURVIVES WILL PROSPER, BE IT A SINGLE BEE...
NARADATTA, THE SMALLER ONES ARE ALL DEAD! AN' THE BIGGER ONES ARE DRAGGING SOMETHING FROM THE OTHERS' HIVE.

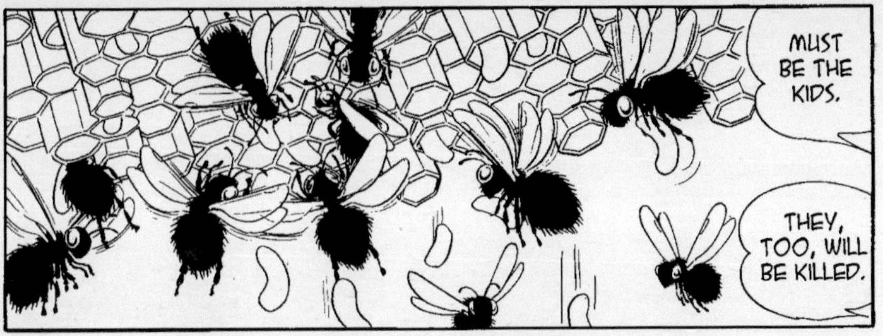
MUST BE THE KIDS.
THEY, TOO, WILL BE KILLED.

BUT THEY DIDN'T DO ANYTHING WRONG...

HEY! NOW THEY'VE FOUND ONE WITH A BIG BELLY!
THAT'S SURELY THE QUEEN.

THE QUEEN IS THE LIFE OF A TRIBE. SHE WILL BE SHOVED, PULLED, AND ABUSED. KEEP YOUR EYES OPEN, BOY.

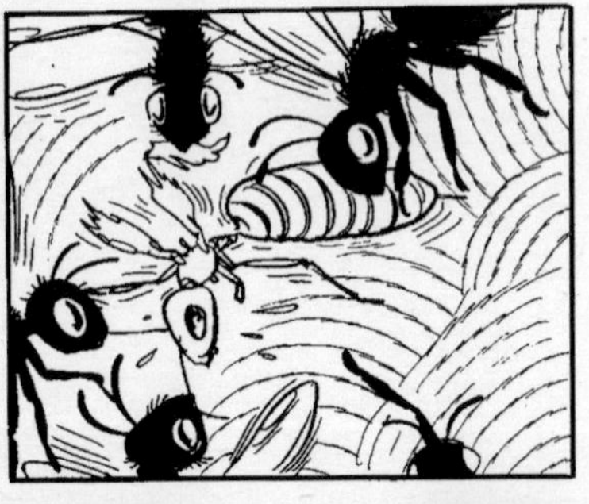

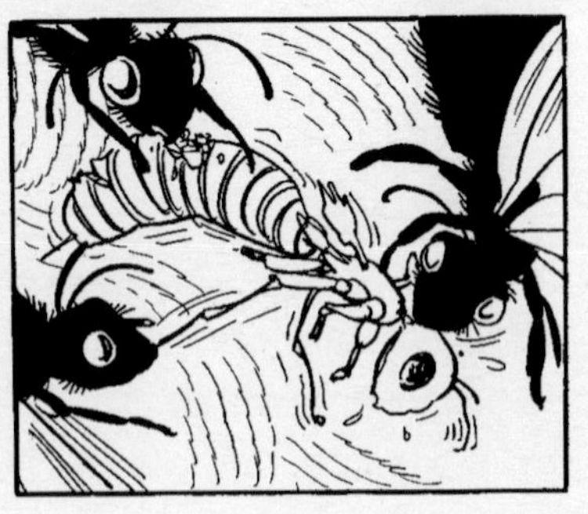

THEY TORE HER TO PIECES.
NOW PEACE WILL REIGN. THE WEAK PERISH, THE STRONG SURVIVE. HEAR THEIR WINGS HUM LOUD WITH TRIUMPH!
WHAT YOU SAW IS CUSTOM FOR ALL LIFE. NO, HUMANS AREN'T EXEMPT. YOU'LL DO WELL TO REMEMBER.
WELL, IT'S SAFE TO MOVE AGAIN. LET'S GO.

THE WEAK PERISH, THE STRONG SURVIVE. CUSTOM FOR ALL LIFE. HUMANS AREN'T EXEMPT.

CHAPTER THREE

THE HAG AND THE WAIF

CAWK

MEOWW!
MEOWW!
UGH
GUH

CAWWW!
GAW GAW
GAWK! GHAW!

HISS

WRAP

CRUNCH
CHOKE
GAG

GAWK
GHAK

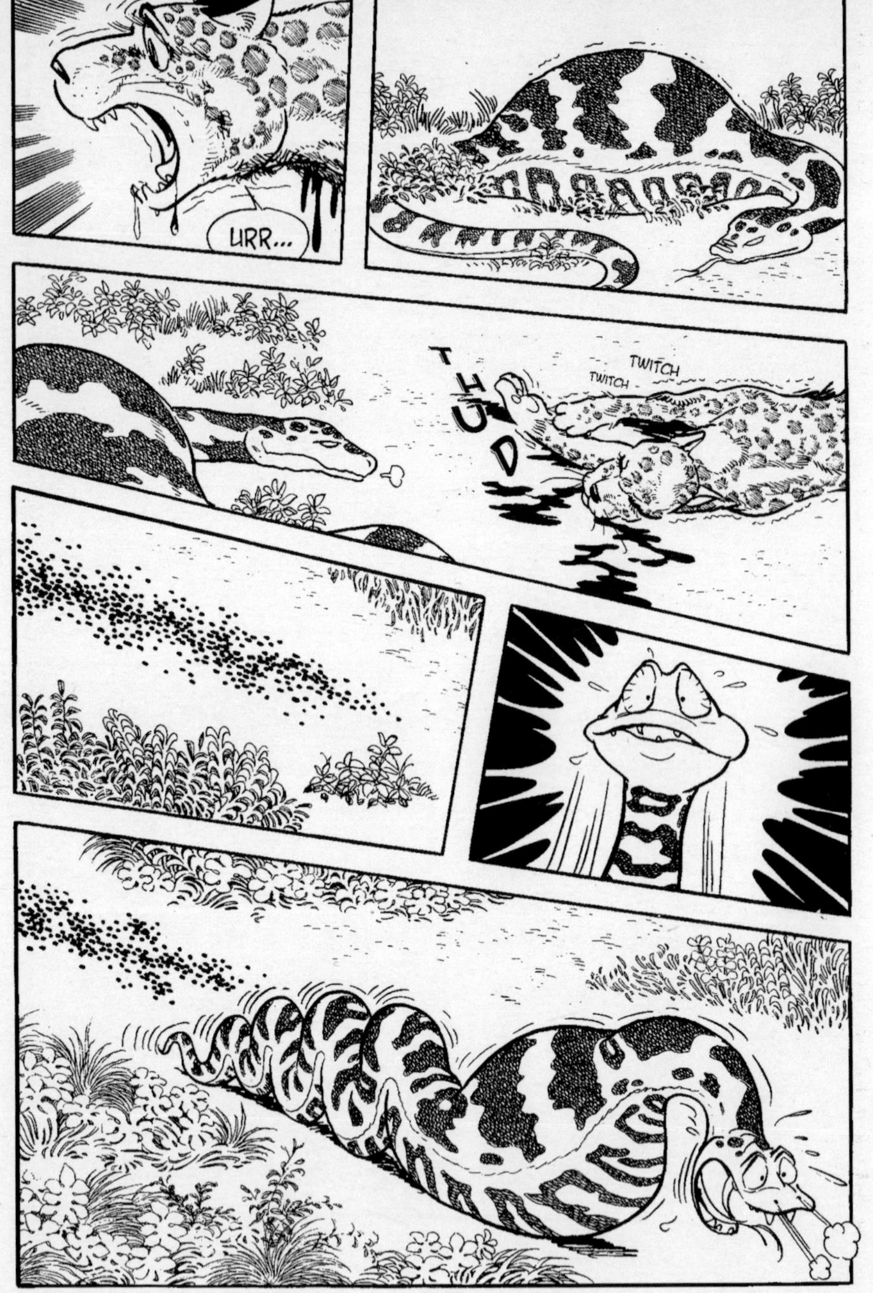
URR...
THUD
TWITCH
TWITCH

RUMBLE RUMBLE
SHHHH

SHHHH
SHHHH
SHHHH
ROAR
ROAR

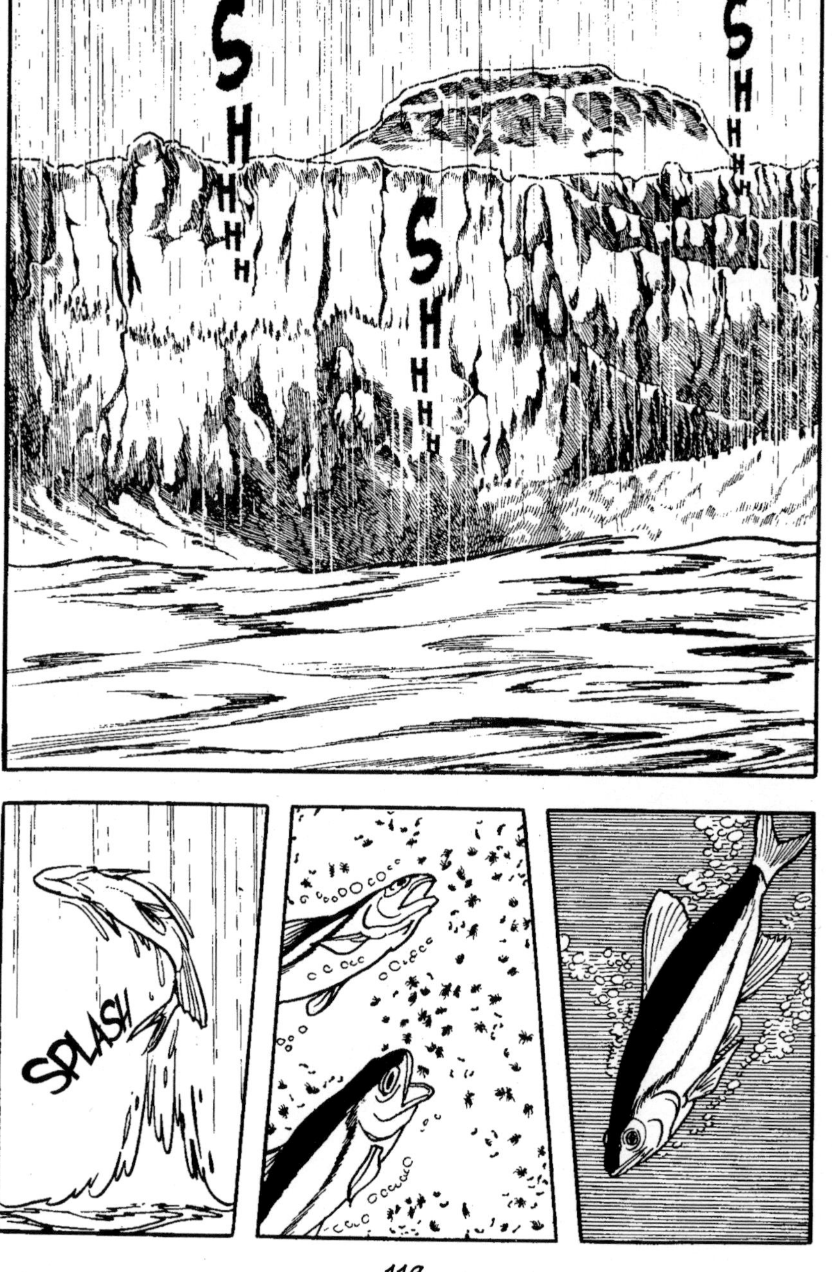
SHHHH
SHHHH
SHHHH
SPLASH

SPLASH

MUNCH
MUNCH
FRISK

NO NEED TO HIDE IT. I KNOW YOU COME HERE IN SECRET TO HUNT AND EAT FISH.
A CHILD OF YOUR AGE IS ALWAYS HUNGRY.
YOU KNEW?

DON'T YOU GET HUNGRY, LIVING ON JUST FRUITS AND NUTS?
I HAVE SWORN NOT TO KILL, NOT EVEN A BUG.

BUT DIDN'T YOU SAY THAT THE STRONG SURVIVE AND THE WEAK PERISH? ISN'T THAT THE LAW OF NATURE?

I CAUGHT THIS FISH.
IT GOT CAUGHT BECAUSE IT'S WEAK. I'M STRONGER THAN IT, SO I CAN EAT IT, RIGHT?

THAT IS THE LOGIC, YES. YOU'RE A SMART BOY.

HEH HEH
YOU DON'T SAY...

BUT YOU ARE QUITE MISTAKEN.
OUCH

THE FISH GOT CAUGHT SO IT COULD BE EATEN.

A FISH GETTING CAUGHT SO IT COULD BE EATEN?!
THAT'S FUNNY! HAHAHA. HAHAHA
IT SOUNDS FUNNY, I'M SURE. I DON'T BLAME YOU FOR LAUGHING.
TONIGHT I'LL EXPLAIN IT ALL TO YOU, HMM?

HA HA HA HA

NO LIVING THING LIVES IN A WORLD...
...ALL ITS OWN. FROM THE TIME IT IS BORN, AND UNTIL IT DIES,

IT
CANNOT
BUT INTERACT
WITH OTHER
LIVING THINGS.
FROM BIRTH
TO DEATH,
EVERY
MOMENT.

TAKE FISH, FOR EXAMPLE. FISH LAY BILLIONS OF EGGS. IF ALL THOSE BILLIONS ACTUALLY SURVIVED

GETTING EATEN BY YOU IS GOOD FOR THEM.

THE WORLD WOULD BE BURIED UNDER FISH. GETTING EATEN BY OTHERS KEEPS THEM AT A GOOD NUMBER.

THE GREAT SKIES AND ALL OF THIS EARTH ARE RULED BY THAT SAME FATE...

TO HAVE CONNECTED EACH AND EVERY THING...

WAIT, NOW. SINCE WHEN HAVE YOU BEEN WALKING ON ALL FOURS?

I WANNA BE LIKE YOU, NARADATTA.

IS THAT WHY?
YOU MUSN'T. I WAS

CONDEMNED TO THE REALM OF BEASTS AS PUNISHMENT. NOT SO FOR YOU.

BUT I LIKE YOU, NARADATTA.
AND I LIKE YOU, TOO, DEVADATTA.
BUT YOU ARE A HUMAN.

THOUGH YOU LIVE OUT HERE, SURELY YOU NEEDN'T CRAWL?
BUT I WANNA

I HATE HUMANS!

DEVADATTA, YOUR WORDS SOUND LIKE A WOLF'S SNARL TO HUMAN EARS, AND NOW, WALKING ON ALL FOURS! NO GOOD CAN COME OF IT.

I DON'T CARE! I'M WOLF ALREADY ANYWAY.

WHAT THE HECK? WHO'S BOY ARE YOU?
RRR
WHAT A SNARL... CREEPY BRAT.
IS HE A WOLF OR WHAT?
JUST LEAVE HIM BE. LET'S CATCH SOME FISH AND BEAT IT.
THIS IS MY TERRITORY!

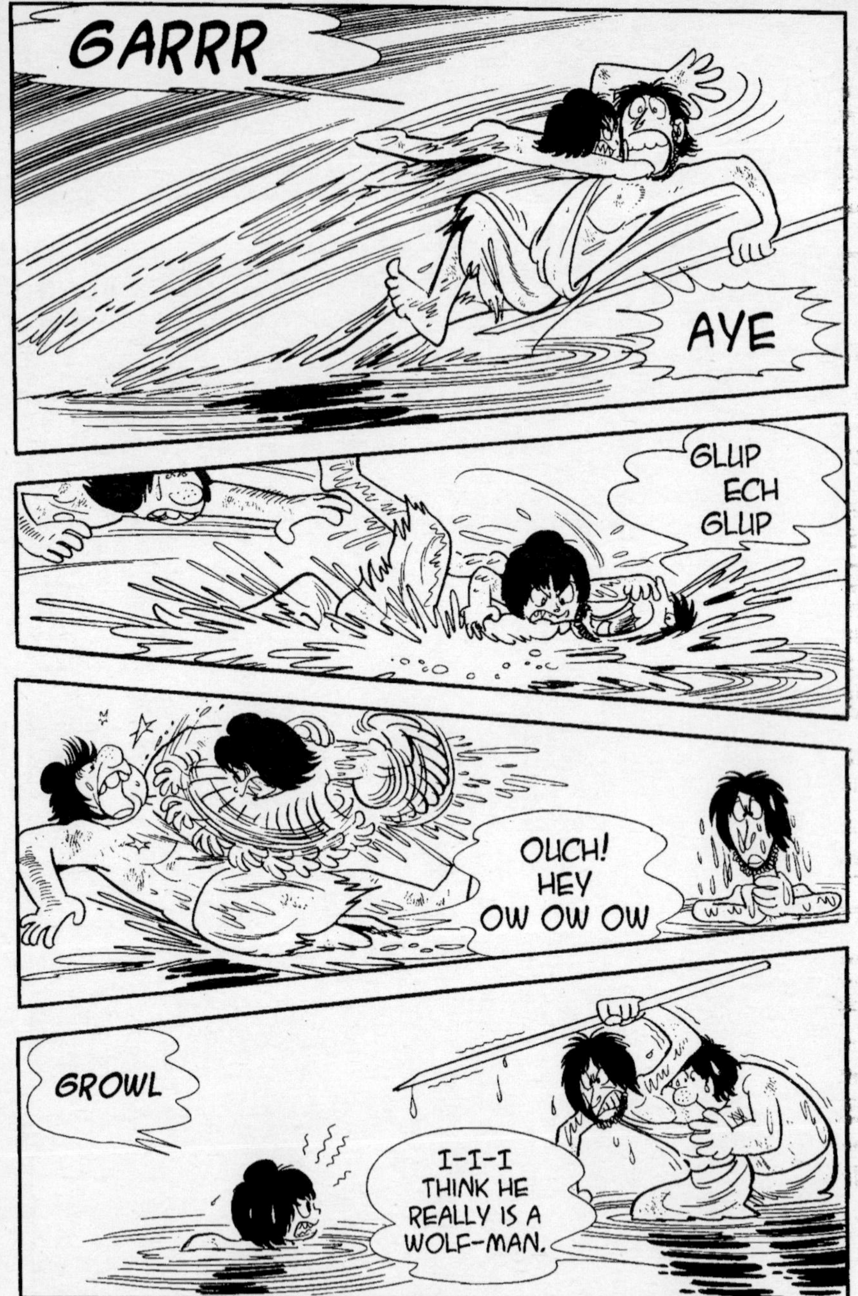
GARRR
AYE
GLUP ECH GLUP
OUCH! HEY OW OW OW
GROWL
I-I-I THINK HE REALLY IS A WOLF-MAN.

PLUSH
SPLOSH
AHHH! OUCH! ARGH!
DAMMIT. DON'T THINK WE'LL FORGET THIS!
HOWL HOWL

WHAT HAVE YOU DONE?!

BUT THEY TRIED TO TAKE MY FISH...

YOU THINK HUMANS EVER BACK DOWN?
THEY'LL KILL YOU!

FAT CHANCE! I'LL WHIP 'EM AGAIN.

CHASE THEM AWAY, THEY RETURN. IT'S NO USE.

LIVING HERE IS GETTING TO BE TOO MUCH FOR YOU.

DEVADATTA, YOU MUST RETURN TO THE HUMAN WORLD.
IN THE LONG RUN, THAT'LL SERVE YOU BETTER.
LET US PART HERE.
NO
NO!!

LISTEN TO ME. WHEN I WAS STILL HUMAN, I LONG SOUGHT A MAN WHOM, ALAS, I NEVER FOUND --

A MAN WHO IS DESTINED TO BECOME A GOD, OR PERHAPS A GREAT RULER, ACCORDING TO MY MASTER.

YOU MUST FIND AND SERVE HIM.
THIS IS A MAN WHO MAY HAVE ANSWERS TO ALL THE RIDDLES OF THE WORLD.

I'M NOT GOING ANYWHERE! I'LL DO ANYTHING, NARADATTA! SO PLEASE LET ME STAY!!
DON'T BE A FOOL.

I SAID NO! NO WAY! NO, NO, NO, NO! TRY TO THROW ME OUT, AND I'LL TEAR YOU TO SHREDS!
WHAT AM I TO DO WITH YOU...?

YOU'RE BOUND TO HAVE A RUN-IN WITH HUMANS. WHEN YOU DO, DON'T COME CRYING TO ME!

HA! NOW YOU FEIGN SLEEP.
DID YOU HEAR WHAT I SAID?

THE WEAK PERISH, BUT THE STRONG SURVIVE... NARADATTA DOESN'T KNOW JUST HOW STRONG I AM! HEH HEH HEH

SNIFF

SNIFF SNIFF

GOTCHA, YUMMY RABBIT!
THUD
GROWL

HOOT

SCRABBLE
SCRABBLE

HOWL
HOWL
HOWL

WHY WON'T YOU COME AND HELP ME?
I KNOW YOU'RE THERE!!

CAN'T YOU HEAR ME?

NARADATTA, YOU'VE COME FOR ME! I CAN SMELL YOU! HURRY AND HELP ME!

HOWL HOWL
GET ME OUTTA HERE! HELP! HELP ME!

I'VE COME TO BID ADIEU.
THAT TRAP WON'T KILL YOU. I'M SURE THE VILLAGERS WILL TURN YOU BACK INTO A HUMAN.
AND A FINE HUMAN AT THAT, I HOPE.

HOWL
HOWL

GATHER ROUND, FOLKS!
WE HAVE HERE, CAPTURED UPSTREAM AT THE FOOT OF THE SACRED MOUNTAIN, A GENUINE WOLF-MAN!!

IT SPEAKS NO HUMAN TONGUE, EMITTING WOLFISH HOWLS AND GROWLS!

WHY, IT'S JUST A LITTLE KID!
AH, BUT THE EYES! AND THOSE FANGS!
IT CAN'T BE HUMAN.

WHAT WOLF-MAN IS THIS? IT'S NOT AT ALL LIKE THE MOVIES. YOU KNOW, LIKE, WEREWOLVES?
GRRR ... GRRR
DAMN THEM, THEY'VE JUST KIDNAPPED SOME POOR KID AND ARE MAKING HIM FAKE IT.

HARD TO BELIEVE, I KNOW.
TO DISPEL YOUR DOUBTS, I WILL NOW DISPLAY THE WOLF-MAN AT ITS MOST FIERCE.

THAT WOLF YOU SEE THERE...
SHALL BE SENT INTO THE CAGE.

BEHOLD, A DUEL 'TWIXT WOLF AND WOLF-MAN!
AH, WHICH WILL TEAR WHICH TO PIECES? ONLY THE GODS KNOW...

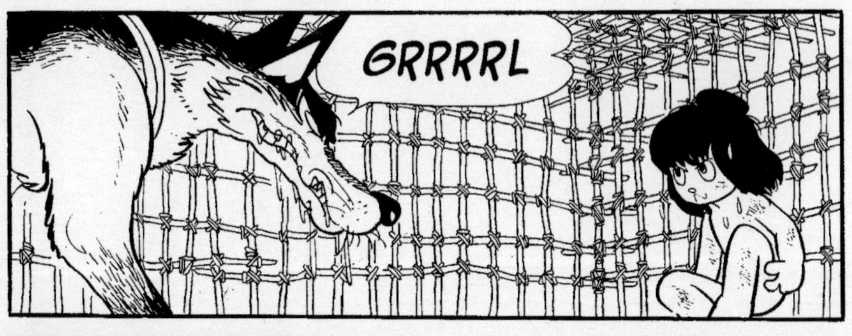
GRRRRL

GRR... GRR...
GIT 'IM!
RIP HIM APART, WOLFIE-BOY, Y'HEAR?

HEY, YOU CALL THIS A FIGHT?
POOH! WE'VE BEEN HAD!
I WANT M'MONEY BACK!
WE AIN'T PAYIN' FOR NO LOVE MATCH!

SNAP
ROAR
YEAH
YES
AARRGH!!
SMACK

MURDER!! SOMEBODY!
ALL RIGHT! IT'S BROKEN FREE!
FOOL, IT'S PART OF THE SHOW.
GRRR
OH, MAN! HE'S BEEN PIERCED BAD.
WATCH OUT!
AHHH!
HE-HE-HELP
AAAY!

GHRRRR
WOOOORF
AHH
AHH
SHOOT TO KILL! KILL THEM BOTH!
WHIZZ
GRRAA... ...
u-u-u...
WHOOSH
WHISH

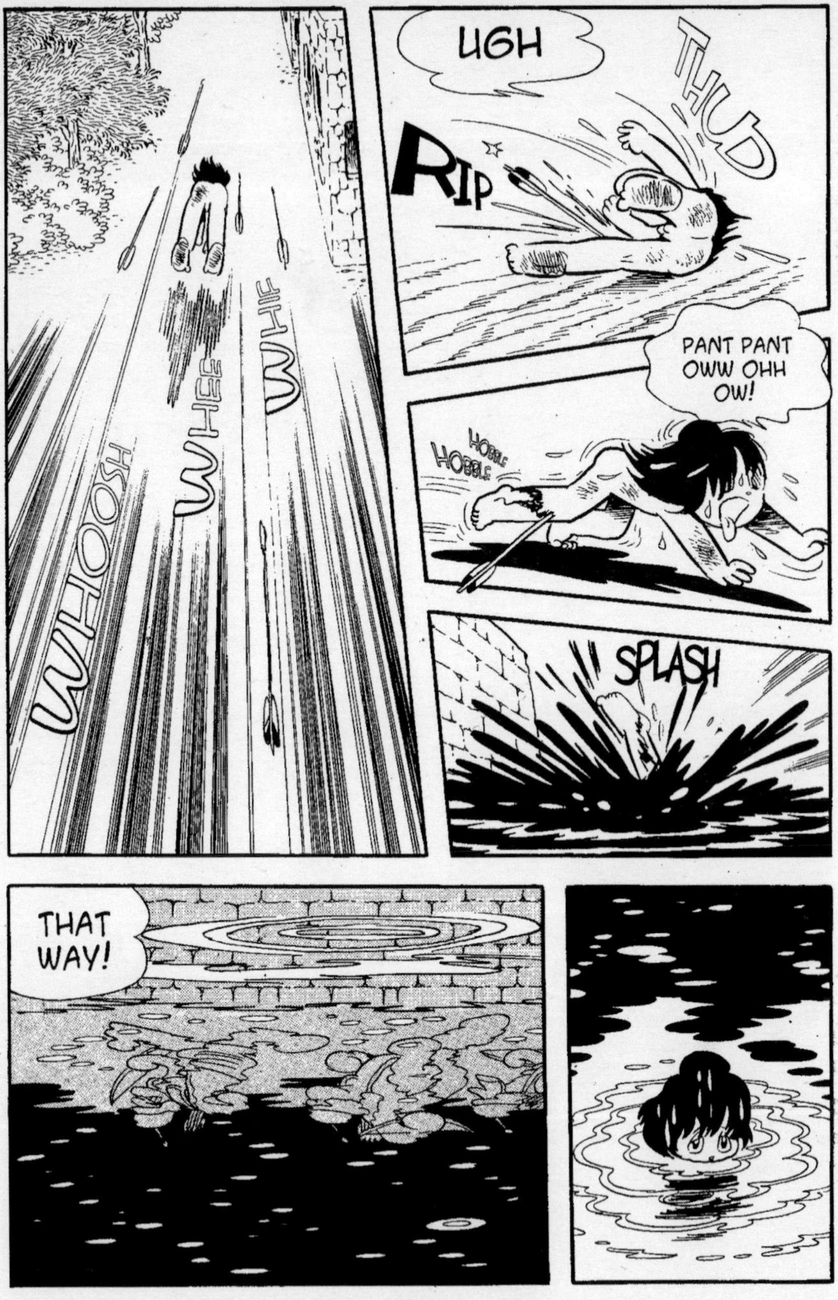

WHOOSH
WHEE
WHIF
UGH
RIP
THUD
PANT PANT OWW OHH OW!
HOBBLE
HOBBLE
SPLASH

LICK LICK
UHH!
DARN GOOD MEAT, THIS.
BITE
URRR
SLURP SLURP

WHAT IN THE WORLD ARE YOU UP TO, KID?
GRRR GRR GRRH
GRR GRR GRRA GRRA
GARR
ECK
YOU DARE ATTACK ME WHILE I'M EATING? EAT THIS!
AAY AHH
ULP

PANT
PANT

HN?!

GROWL!
WOOF!
BAA
BAA
BAA

WHAM
BONK
THWACK

COUGH...
COUGH...

THE WEAK PERISH,
THE STRONG SURVIVE...
TRUE FOR ALL LIFE...
HUMANS NO EXCEPTION...

DIRTY LITTLE GOAT THIEF! GET LOST ALREADY!

BASH

HAA HAA

SNIFF

WHINE
WHINE

CLUNK
BONK
POK

HEY KID!
WILL YA STOP PEEKING INTO MY HOME?

GO BEG SOMEONE ELSE!

WHIMPER

DRINK UP NOW...

AND GO TO SLEEP.

ROCK-A-BY BA-BY... ... IN THE... TREETOP...

... ...

MISTER FOX IS FAST ASLEEP. LAP YOUR MILK AND GET SOME SLEEP.

ZZZ
ZZZ

ZZZZZZ

ZZ

Slurp

Slurp
Slurp

AIEEE

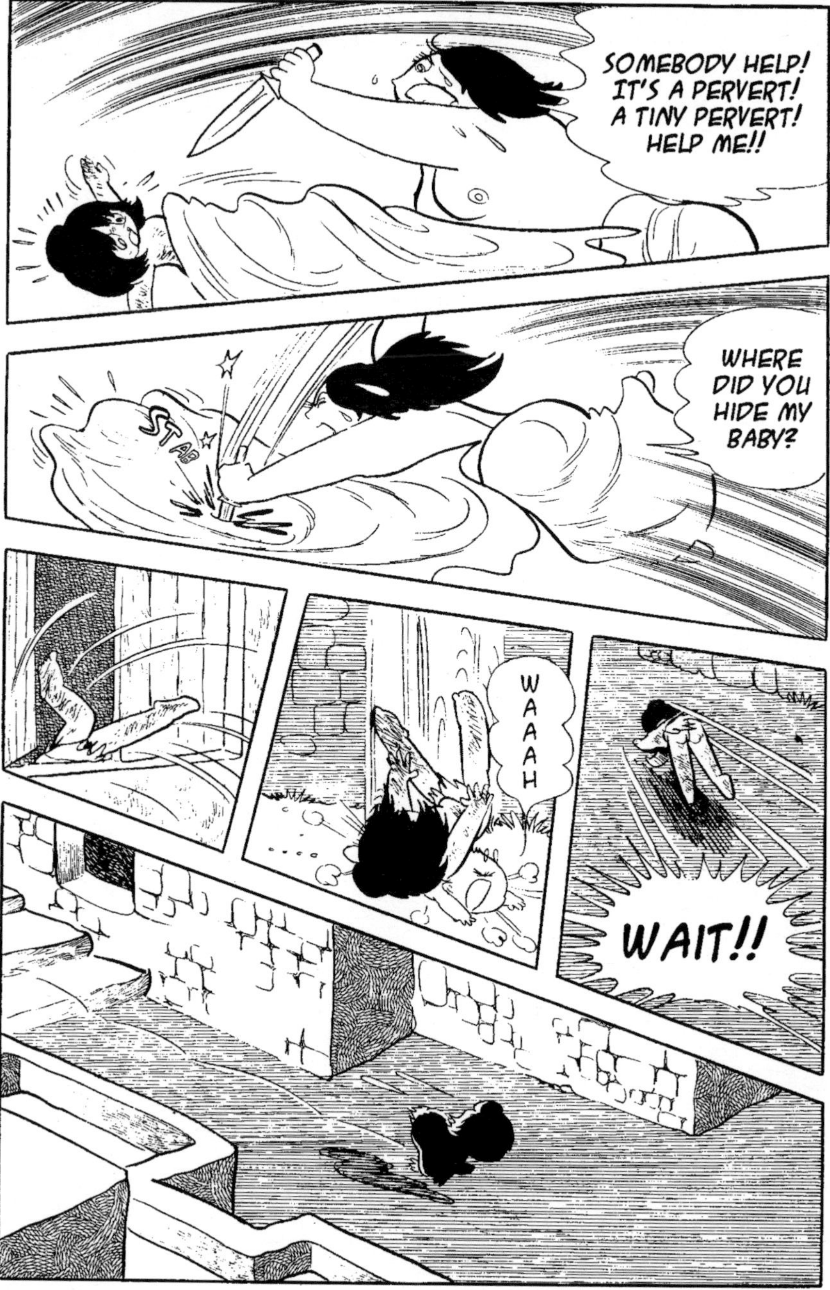
SOMEBODY HELP! IT'S A PERVERT! A TINY PERVERT! HELP ME!!
WHERE DID YOU HIDE MY BABY?
STAB
WAAAH
WAIT!!

HAA HAA HAA HAA
WHO GOES THERE? A THIEF COME TO PLY HIS TRADE, OR A BEGGAR BOWING DEEP? NEITHER'S WELCOME.

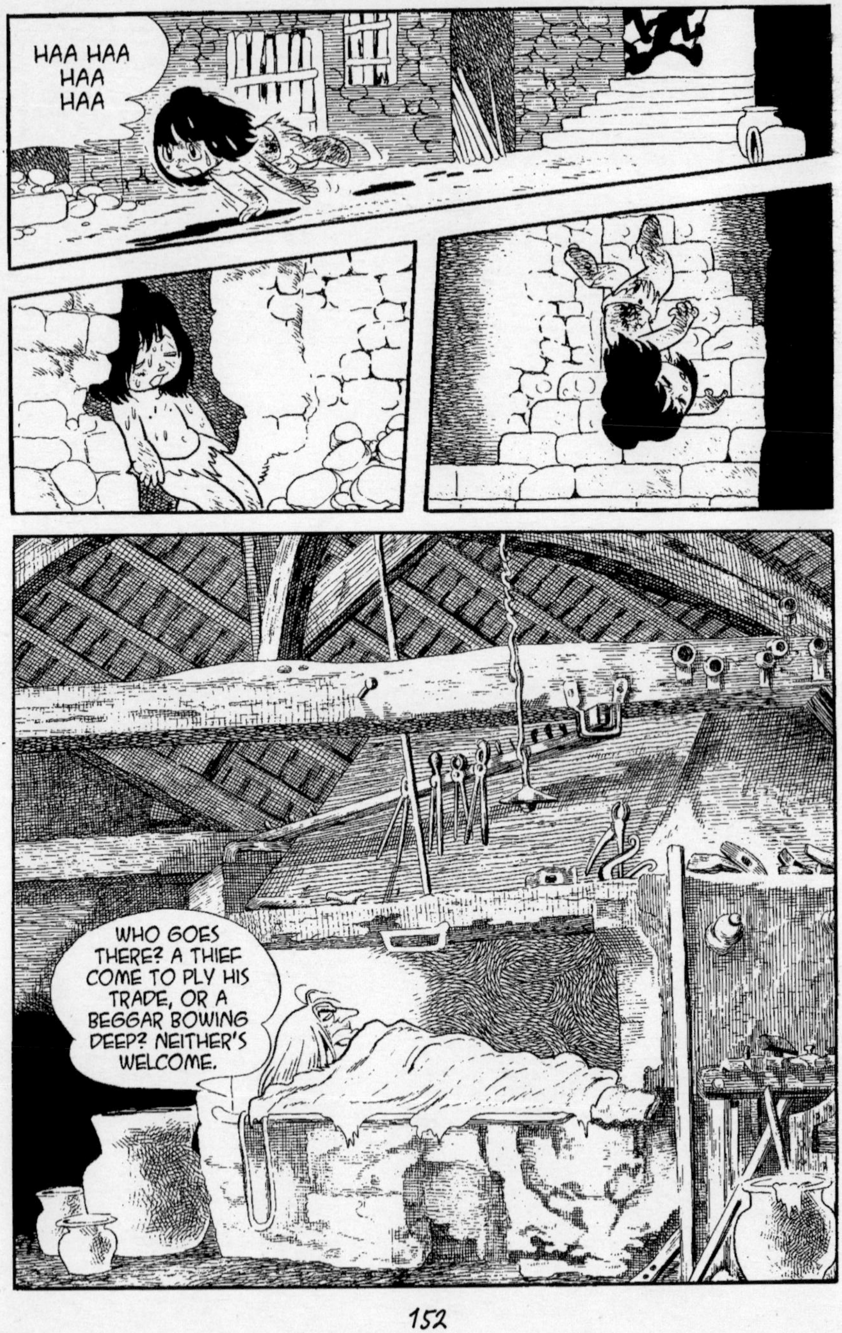

?

HUMPH! A BOY, A LITTLE BOY.

EHH... COVERED IN BLOOD? HURT, IS HE?
ARE YOU SHUDRA (SLAVE)?
SPEAK TO ME.
GRR

WELL, I HAVE OINT-MENT.

THERE, PUT IT ON YOURSELF.

WEIRD BOY JUST LICKS THE SALVE, DOES HE?

HERE, I'LL DO IT FOR YOU. COME, COME.

NARY A WORD...

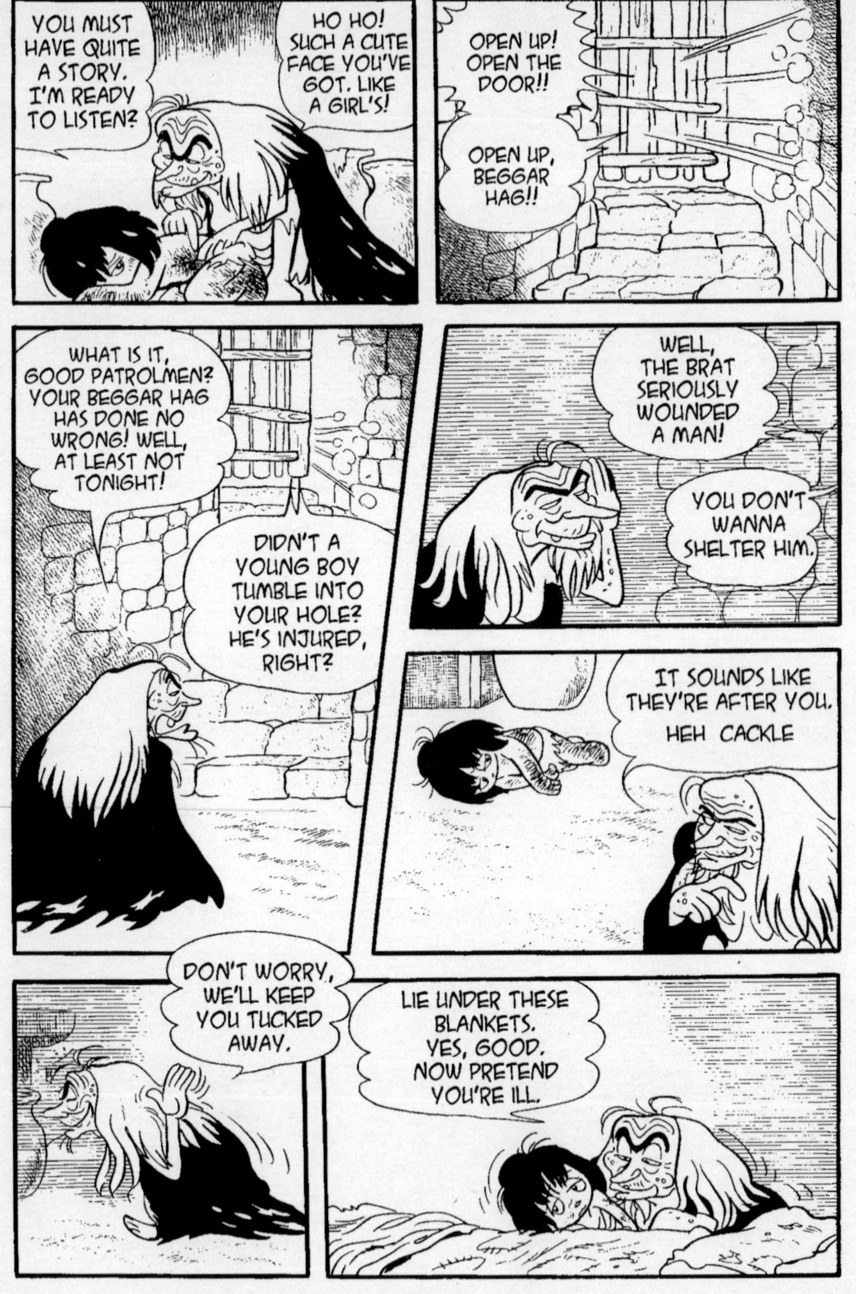
YOU MUST HAVE QUITE A STORY. I'M READY TO LISTEN?
HO HO! SUCH A CUTE FACE YOU'VE GOT. LIKE A GIRL'S!
OPEN UP! OPEN THE DOOR!!
OPEN UP, BEGGAR HAG!!
WHAT IS IT, GOOD PATROLMEN? YOUR BEGGAR HAG HAS DONE NO WRONG! WELL, AT LEAST NOT TONIGHT!
DIDN'T A YOUNG BOY TUMBLE INTO YOUR HOLE? HE'S INJURED, RIGHT?
WELL, THE BRAT SERIOUSLY WOUNDED A MAN!
YOU DON'T WANNA SHELTER HIM.
IT SOUNDS LIKE THEY'RE AFTER YOU.
HEH CACKLE
DON'T WORRY, WE'LL KEEP YOU TUCKED AWAY.
LIE UNDER THESE BLANKETS. YES, GOOD. NOW PRETEND YOU'RE ILL.

COME IN, COME IN!

OPEN THIS!
WE'RE GONNA SEARCH YOUR PLACE, OKAY?

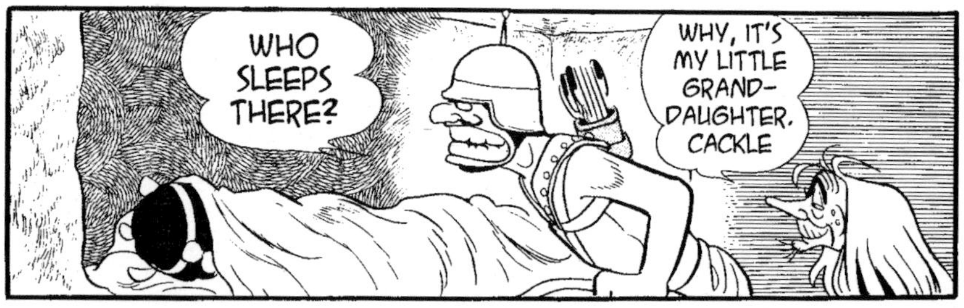
WHO SLEEPS THERE?
WHY, IT'S MY LITTLE GRAND-DAUGHTER. CACKLE

SINCE WHEN HAVE YOU HAD A GRANDCHILD? CUT THE CRAP, WILL YOU?
TONIGHT'S NOT THE NIGHT TO BE RUDE TO ME, IS IT? WHY SHOULDN'T I HAVE ONE?

YIKES!

LET'S LOOK ELSE-WHERE.
CACKLE... THE RUSE WORKED.

SO YOU STABBED A MAN, EH? WHAT AN OUTRAGEOUS BOY.
OR RATHER, A PROMISING ONE.

MY NAME IS GHAGRA.
I MAY NOT LOOK IT, BUT I WAS ONCE THE WIFE OF A RICH MAN, HERE IN THIS VERY COUNTRY.

MY MAN CAST ME ASIDE, LIKE A PIECE OF TRASH, TO BETTER HIS LOT.
HE NEEDED TO MARRY A GIRL RELATED TO THE ROYAL CLAN, AND SO HE DID!

I CURSED HIM! I CURSED THE WOMAN, TOO! I SWORE I WOULD ROB THEM OF ALL THEY HAD, AND THEREBY AVENGE MYSELF, EVEN IF IT TOOK ME A LIFETIME.

BUT LOOK AT ME NOW,
DECREPIT. I CAN NO LONGER PULL IT OFF BY MYSELF.

PERHAPS YOU WERE BROUGHT HERE BY HEAVENLY DESIGN. NAY, I AM SURE OF IT!
YOU SPEAK NOT A WORD. SO MUCH THE BETTER.

THIS IS POISON, OF MY OWN BREWING.

I MADE IT FROM WOLFS-BANE ROOT!
WHOEVER DRINKS IT SLEEPS THE SLEEP OF THE DEAD.
AS YOU ARE BLESSED WITH FEMININE FEATURES...
I SHALL SELL YOU AS A FEMALE SLAVE...
TO THE HOUSE OF MY NEMESIS!
YOUR FIRST TARGET SHALL BE...
THEIR FOOL OF A SON.
YOU WILL WIN HIS HEART.
CHARM HIM FIRST, THEN GO FOR THE
KILL!
WHAT? SCARED? YOU WILL NOT DO MY BIDDING?!

HO! HO HO! A BEAUTY! WHAT A FETCHING MAIDEN!
RISE AND BEHOLD YOURSELF IN THE MIRROR. CHARMING, EHH?

WHAT IS THIS?!
CAN'T YOU EVEN STAND ON TWO FEET? RISE, I SAID! RISE!
WHIP!
CRAWLING LIKE A BABE!
LASH
UH ... UH
YOU GOOD-FOR-NOTHING!
LISTEN WELL. IF YOU BUNGLE THIS YOU WILL DRINK THAT POISON YOURSELF.

FROM TOMORROW ON,
I'LL DRILL YOU IN A WOMAN'S WAYS.

ENOUGH. SLEEP THERE ON THE FLOOR.

OH-HO... WHAT FOND MEMORIES. THIS USED TO BE MY HOME.

THAT'S HIM! THE BESOTTED SON OF THE WOMAN I LOATHE.
NOW GO FORTH, SWAYING LITHELY.
WHOA! IF SHE ISN'T A CUTIE!
WHOSE SLAVE ARE YOU?
YOU'RE MY TYPE, Y'KNOW THAT?
...
I'M BUYING! YOU'RE TO BE MY PERSONAL SERVANT, HEH HEH.
...
SMOOCH

...

SAY SOMETHING.

NOT A WORD! YOU'RE A QUIET ONE, AREN'T YOU?

TALK, AND THIS IS YOURS...

THOUGH I HATE TO PART WITH IT.

...

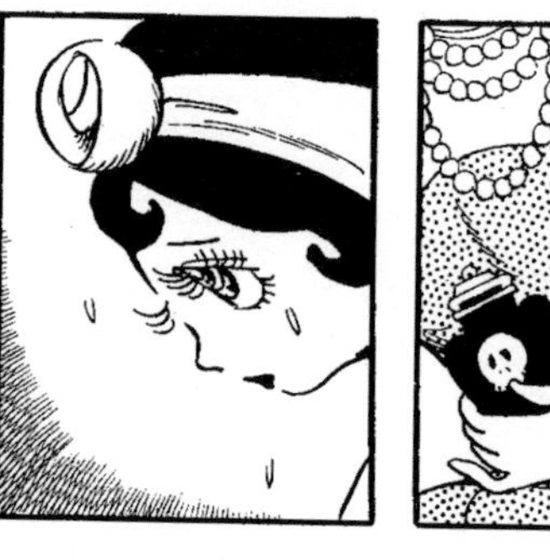

THE F-FISH... ALL GONE BELLY UP!

...P-P-POISON?!

THE POND'S BEEN FOULED...
YOU...!
HIEEE!
UH
BLOMP
SOMEBODY HELP ME! SA-SAS-SASS-ASSASSIN! HELP ME!!

TH-THE GIRL... P-P-P-POISON.
YOUNG MASTER?
THERE SHE IS! CATCH HER!
SOME VILLAIN POSING AS A SLAVE GIRL TRIED TO DO ME IN! SOMEBODY HELP ME OUTTA HERE!
SPLASH
AH
WHAT THE - ? SHE'S RUNNING ON ALL FOURS!

'TWAS NO MAIDEN. A WILD DOG?!
NEVER DID SAY A WORD!

YOU GO SEARCH THAT WAY.

...

BAM!
PITPAT

AH, MY LAD! TELL ME ALL.

YOU LOUT !!
CRACK
DUNCE!!
CRACK
ALL MY CAREFUL SCHEMING! ALL MY FINE, HARD WORK DISGUISING YOU AS A MAIDEN, AND SCHOOLING YOU IN FEMININE WILES!
WHIP
WHAT A BUNGLER !!

LASH
CRACK
CRACK
WHIP
SO YOU SWIPED THIS?
...I'LL LET YOU OFF FOR TODAY.
BUT NEXT TIME YOU SCREW UP, LAD, DON'T EXPECT TO BE FORGIVEN.
NOW GO TO SLEEP!!
... ...
CACKLE TEE-HEE

TEE HEE

COME HERE, HAND-SOME!

BOOGIE WOOGIE! SWING IT!

TA-TA-TA TA-TA-TA LA LA LA LA LA LA LA!

DEVADATTA'S EYES OPENED WIDE WITH ASTONISHMENT; EAGER FOR A CLUE, HE STARED AND STARED AT THE OLD HAG. JUST WHAT HAD MADE HER SO DELIRIOUSLY HAPPY?

IT WAS THOSE TINY STONES THAT HAD ENCHANTED HER! AND SO DID YOUNG DEVADATTA LEARN OF THE MAGICAL POWER OF GEMS.

WHOA, GRANDMA! WHO'D YA RELIEVE OF THIS PRICEY ITEM? WITH YOUR RUSTY OLD TRICKS, TOO!
HURRY AND NAME YOUR PRICE. IT'S WORTH AT LEAST 30,000!

...AH, BUT IF IT'S HOT, I TAKE THE HEAT... CAN'T SHELL OUT MORE THAN 2,000.

ONLY?! SCOUNDREL, YOU'D TAKE ADVANTAGE OF A –
TAKE IT OR LEAVE IT.

THERE, 2K!

DON'T JUST STARE! GIVE ME A HAND!

HMM, ALMOST FORGOT...

WANT ONE? YOU'D LIKE ONE, TOO? HERE, BOY.
?

!

...

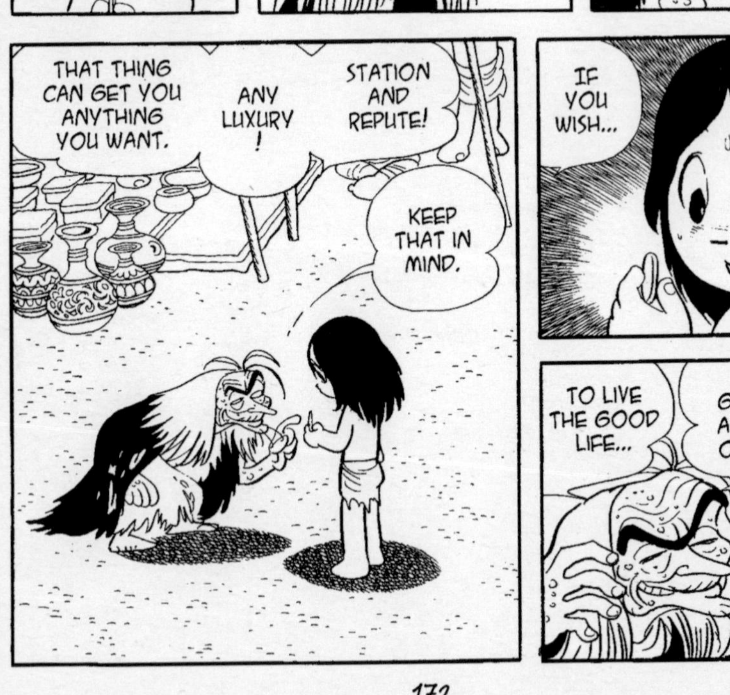

IF YOU WISH...

TO LIVE THE GOOD LIFE...
GET PILES AND PILES OF THAT!

YESTERDAY: TINY STONES... TODAY: THIS SHINY DISC! OWNING MANY OF THESE "COINS" MAKES YOU A HAPPY PERSON... BUT WHY?
COULD THE DISC IN HIS HANDS REALLY HOLD SO MUCH POWER? THAT SEEMED UNLIKELY...THE HUMAN WORLD WAS BIZARRE! IT WAS... INSANE.
COME
BLEAGH

LIKE IT?
MONEY ALSO BUYS YOUTH AND BEAUTY.
GAG

BARF
WHAT'S WRONG WITH YOU?
I'M GOING TO A HIGH-CLASS RESTAURANT. THAT'S WHY I'M ALL DRESSED UP.

I'LL SHOW THEM THAT I'M...
EVERY BIT AS CLASSY AS I USED TO BE IN THE OLDEN DAYS!

NARADATTA SAID HE REALLY WANTED TO RETURN ME TO THE HUMAN WORLD... I HATE IT HERE! THE WILDS WERE A HUNDRED TIMES BETTER. MAYBE I'LL GO BACK.

MONEY...! HAVING LOTS OF MONEY MAKES YOU STRONG, IN THE PEOPLE WORLD. OR SO SAYS THE OLD WOMAN. I WONDER IF I'D BECOME STRONG, TOO, IF I GATHERED MORE...

TUMBLE
THUNK

PAMPERED ME AS LONG AS I WAS DOLING OUT THE CASH...

BUT ONCE MY PURSE WAS EMPTY, IT WAS, "GET LOST, HAG!"

CURSE THEM!

BOO, HOO, HOOO

BOO, HOO, HOO...

I KNOW !!

WE'LL GET MORE MONEY!

I'LL SHOW THE ONES WHO THREW ME OUT THAT THEY MADE A BIG MISTAKE.

MY LAD, GO BACK TO THAT MANSION.

BUT THIS TIME, NOT AS A MAIDEN. GET HIRED AS A GARDENER!
YOU KNOW THE MANSION WELL NOW... GO TEND THEIR GARDEN, WAIT FOR YOUR CHANCE...
THEN SNEAK INTO THAT BITCH'S CHAMBER AND STEAL HER GEMS. HEE, HEE!

AND WHILE YOU'RE AT IT, MIX SOME POISON IN HER FOOD.

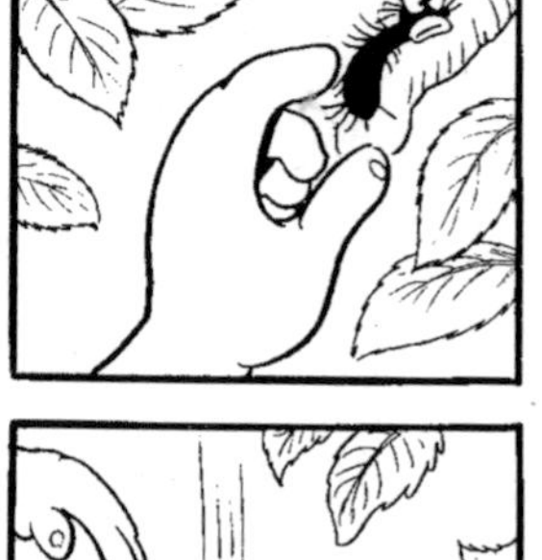

HMM, I SEE HE'S GOT SOME SPINE...
BETTER LEARN TO LIKE BUGS IF YOU'RE GOING TO GARDEN...
ALLLL RIGHT! DON'T MISS ANY!

BAG THEM ALL AND WE'LL BURN...

PUFF!!

ECK

HMM
YOU REMIND ME OF SOMEONE.

THINK NOW.
WHO WAS IT?

LET ME SEE YOU AGAIN.

WORMS !!
AAAAAAAY
PHEW
HOP
AT YER SER- VICE

MOMMY!

IT'S NOT MOMMY, BUT SHE SMELLS THE SAME.

I'VE NEVER SEEN SUCH A PRETTY, SWEET-SMELLING WOMAN.
GRANNY REALLY WANTS ME TO KILL THIS BEAUTIFUL HUMAN?
I WISH I DIDN'T HAVE TO DO IT...

...
PLOP
PLOP

OHHH

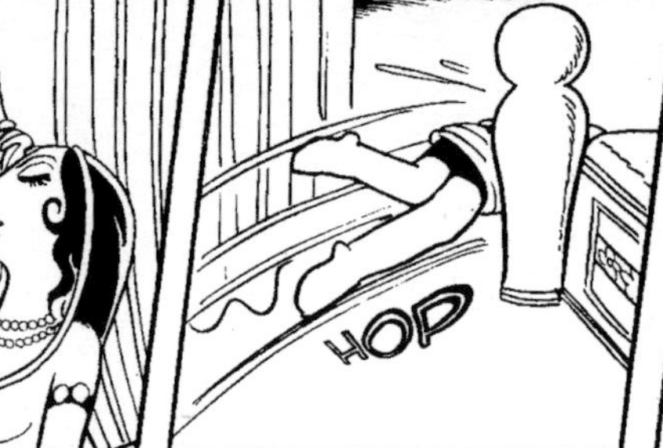
HOP

I THOUGHT I HEARD SOMETHING?

AHH!!
CLANK!!

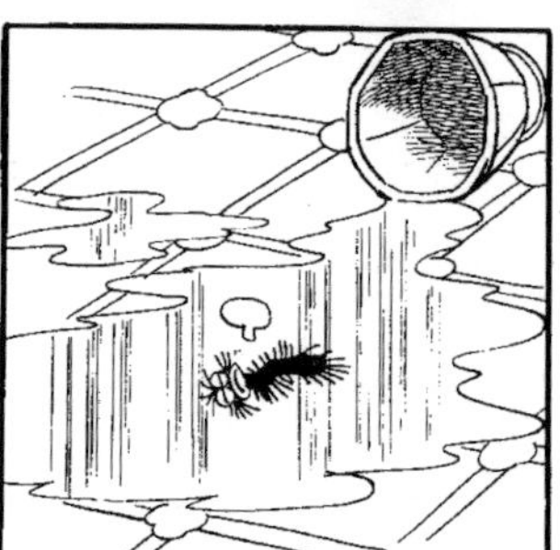

WHO ARE YOU?
WHO HIDES THERE?

...
...
COME OUT, I WON'T BITE YOU. DON'T BE AFRAID.

YOU WORK IN OUR GARDEN, RIGHT?

HMM... DID YOU COME IN THROUGH THE WINDOW?

HA HA, YOU'RE KIND OF CUTE! WHY, YOU LOOK PRETTY CLEVER, TOO.
YOU DON'T SEEM LIKE A BAD BOY.

BUT TELL ME: WHY DID YOU PUT THAT CATERPILLAR IN MY GOBLET? SPEAK UP!!
...

I WON'T HAVE MISCHIEF.
IF YOU'VE A REASON, TELL ME.

NOW SAY SOMETHING !
WHAT'S THAT YOU'VE GOT HIDDEN IN YOUR HAND? SHOW ME!

HURRY UP AND SHOW IT TO ME.

POI SON

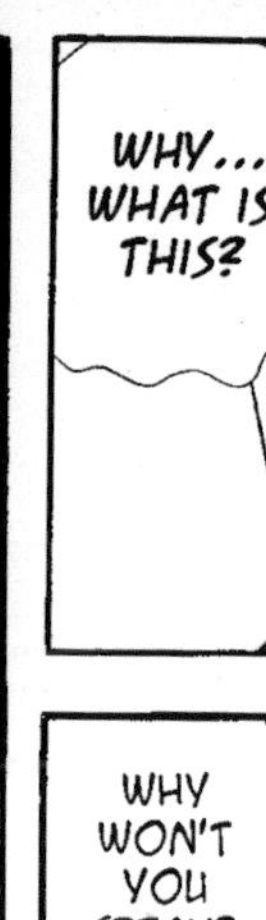
WHY... WHAT IS THIS?

WHY WON'T YOU SPEAK?
ARE YOU DUMB?

HAVE YOU COME TO KILL ME?
HOW... HORRIBLE!

BUT WHY THE CATER-PILLAR?

...AND NOT THE POISON?

M...MOMMY

"MOMMY" DID YOU SAY?
LIKE MOMMY ...

I SEE!
YOU COULDN'T KILL ME BECAUSE I REMINDED YOU OF YOUR MOTHER.

SO YOU ARE A SWEET BOY, AFTER ALL. WHICH MEANS YOU'LL TELL ME WHO GAVE YOU THE POISON.

SEE... I'LL REWARD YOU...
CLINK
CLINK

NOW TELL ME.
G...G... GHA... ...GRA...

VERY WELL, THANK YOU.
YOU'RE A GOOD BOY.
NOW TAKE THAT AND BE GONE!

GHAGRA, IS IT? SO MY HUSBAND'S EX HAS BEEN TRYING TO KILL ME USING A KID! THINK AGAIN, BITCH!

GUARDS, QUICK!

TRAIL THAT CHILD WHO JUST LEFT. FIND OUT WHERE HE LIVES, AND KILL EVERYONE THERE. THE CHILD, TOO, OF COURSE.

YOU
WANT
OIL?

WAIT, WHAT'S HE UP TO?
SOME CRAP.

SPLASH

BOOM
DAMMIT! THE WHOLE STREET'S ABLAZE!!

SHIT, PAL... WE'VE BEEN HAD.
PANT
PANT
PANT
G... GHA... GRA
WUF WUF GRR GRR GR-WUF OOF

HUH?

GHA...GRA...K-KILL COMING!...NOW!!
WHAAAAT?

BUNGLED IT AGAIN, DID YOU, NINCOMPOOP! AND NOW THEY'RE AFTER YOU, IS THAT IT?
TELL ME IN WORDS! WHAT NOW?

RUN NOW... FAST

WHAT A FIASCO !!

I I I'M TOO OLD TOO OLD TO BE RUN-RUNNING LIKE THIS!
WHEEZ
WHEEZ

A HORSE WAGON! THE GODS MUST BE ON MY SIDE!
WHIP
GIT, GIT! GIDDYAP GIDDYAP!
RATTLE RATTLE RATTLE
CLUCK! CLUCK-CLUCK!
BEGGAR HAG PASS THIS WAY?
JUST FLEW OUT THAT GATE.
AFTER THEM!

CRACK
LAD! RUB MY SHOULDERS! THEY'RE GETTING STIFF.
OOF WUF
DAMMIT... I WON'T LET THEM SLAUGHTER ME. THEY WILL NEVER CATCH GHAGRA!

GALLOP
GALLOP
WUF OOOF
...
WHINE
WHINE
WHINE
UH...
SLITHER

LOOKS LIKE IT'S OVER FOR ME.
CAN'T EVEN MUSTER THE WILL TO STAND. D'RATHER REST... FOREVER.

'TIS THE ONLY THING
THAT NO PILE OF GOLD'S EVER FIXED.

YOU'RE STILL YOUNG. LAD... WHEN YOU GROW UP, YOU'LL SEE HOW LIFE MAKES YOU VILE. VILE.

IN THE END WE ALL MUST DIE.
NO USE WAILING ABOUT THAT...

UHH

REALLY WANNA DIE?

UHH... UHH...

ARGHH
HELP! MUR-DER !!!!

COUGH COUGH

GRANNY
GRANNY!

I'D HATE TO DIE LIKE THAT.
IF I HAVE TO BE HUMAN AGAIN...
I WANT TO HAVE A LOT OF MONEY. I'LL BE A STRONG HUMAN, THE STRONGEST ONE ALIVE!

THUS DEVADATTA SET TO WANDER,
A PUPPET OF FATE, HOMELESS
DESPITE HIS NOBLE LINEAGE.
ONE DAY HE WOULD COME UPON
THE SHORES OF THE GANGES,
THAT MAJESTIC FLOW,
AND TRAVEL DOWNSTREAM
AS THOUGH CRADLED TO ITS BOSOM.
--BUT NOT UNTIL SOME TEN YEARS
AFTER SIDDHARTHA'S FIRST
JOURNEY AS A MONK.

CHAPTER FOUR

SUKANDA THE KNIGHT

LET US NOW TURN BACK THE CLOCK AND REJOIN SIDDHARTHA ON HIS JOURNEY.

SHHH

SHHH

SHHH

SHHH
SIDDHARTHA, DON'T LET IT BOTHER YOU.

OH, COME ON!

SHHH
SHHH

HELLO?

I'M SO SORRY!

THERE, I'LL CARRY YOU.
FORGIVE US... IT WAS VERY CRUEL OF US TO JUST MARCH ON AND ABANDON A CHILD LIKE YOU...

YOU'RE BURNING UP.
WHAT A FEVER!

SIDDHARTHA, THIS IS SOME DISEASE, AND HE'S GOING TO GIVE IT TO US.
DO YOU SEE WHY I DON'T WANT SOME KID WITH ME ON THE ROAD?
BUT HE'LL DIE IF WE LEAVE HIM HERE.

ISN'T IT ENOUGH THAT WE HAVE TO CROSS A SEA OF MUD?
DHEPA, YOU GO ON AHEAD. THE CHILD AND I WILL FOLLOW.

NO...I WOULDN'T DO THAT TO YOU.

WE'LL TAKE TURNS.

DUNK
SPLASH
WE'LL SEE HOW FAR WE CAN GO.
A FEW MILES WEST OF HERE IS THE TOWN OF PANDAWA.
SHHH
SHHH
SHHH
SHHH

SHHH
SHHH

WE ARE SAMANNA. PLEASE OPEN THE GATES AND GRANT US SHELTER.
WE HAD TO CROSS A SEA OF MUD, AND THE CHILD IS ILL.

SHHH
SHHH

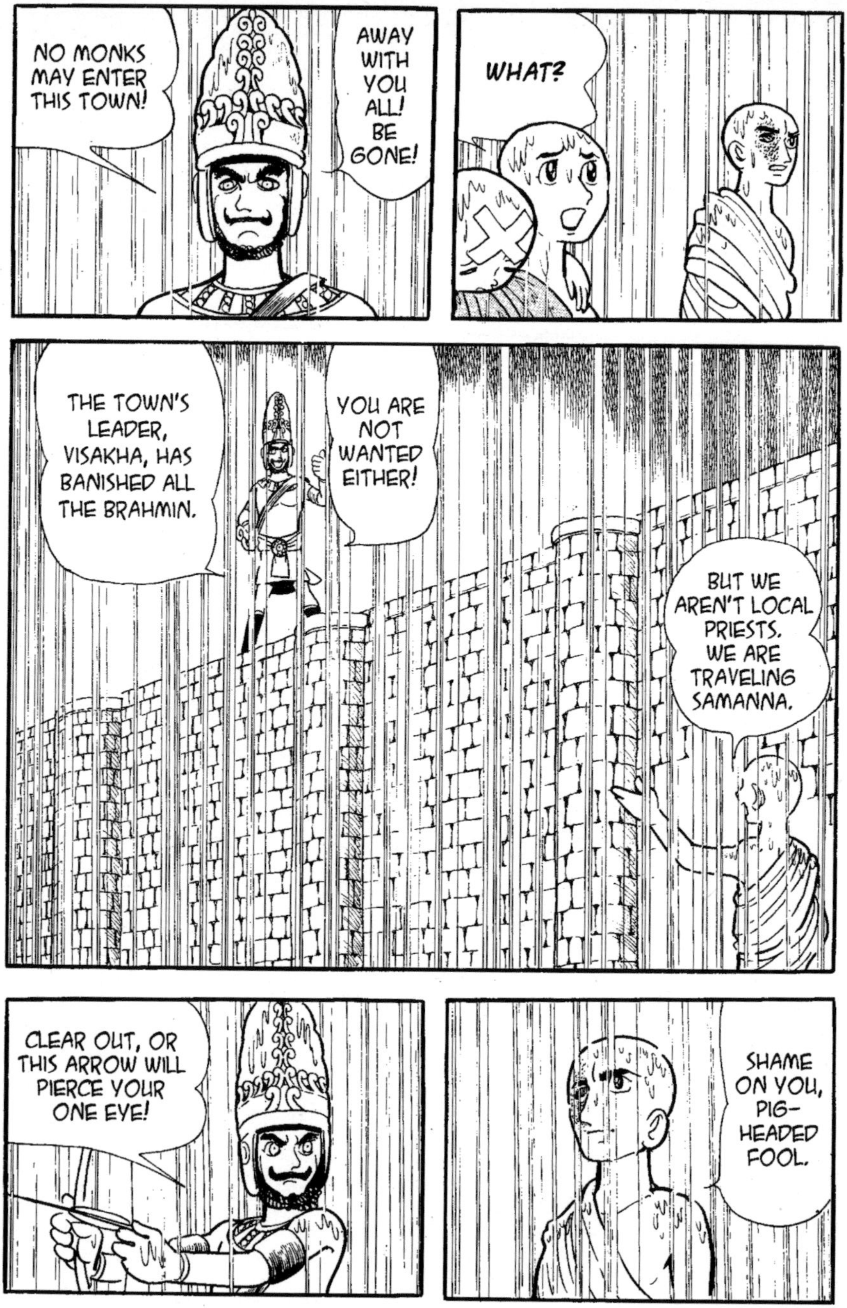

THE TOWN'S LEADER, VISAKHA, HAS BANISHED ALL THE BRAHMIN.

YOU ARE NOT WANTED EITHER!

BUT WE AREN'T LOCAL PRIESTS. WE ARE TRAVELING SAMANNA.

200 LEAGUES HENCE IS THE CAPITAL OF MAGADHA KINGDOM. GO THERE IF YOU NEED ALMS SO BADLY, BEGGAR MONKS!
WE'LL NEVER MAKE IT IN THIS RAIN WITH A SICK CHILD!
DHEPA, THOSE STONES!
HAS HE NO HEART? AH, BUT EVEN SO, I SHAN'T RESENT A MAN.
EASIER SAID THAN DONE... BUT IT BEATS TREKKING TO OUR DEATHS IN THIS DOWNPOUR.
LET'S STACK THEM UP AGAINST THE WALL AND CLIMB TO THE TOP.

HUP, THERE WE GO...
AS USUAL, THE DEED WAS LESS DAUNTING THAN THE THOUGHT OF IT.
LET'S SEE. HOW GOES THE TOWN? ...
LOOK !!
WE DID IT!

...
...

THESE ARE ALL GRAVES!
SOME-THING HAPPEN-ED HERE.

DID I NOT WARN YOU? YET YOU HAVE COME, AS I FEARED.
HOW DO YOU LIKE THIS TOWN, PERFUMED WITH DEATH? HOW DO YOU LIKE THE ROWS OF GRAVES?
AND KNOW THAT YOU HAVE LEFT ME NO CHOICE BUT TO SLAY THAT SICK CHILD OF YOURS.

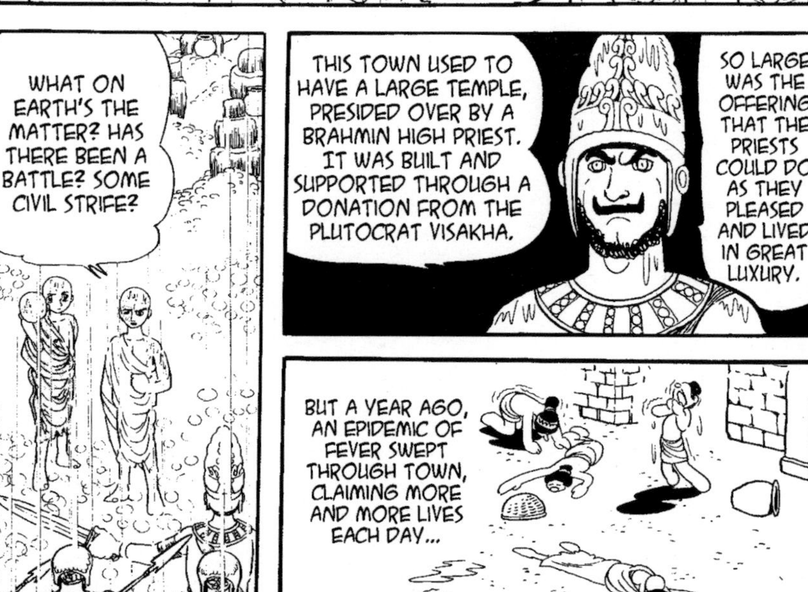
WHAT ON EARTH'S THE MATTER? HAS THERE BEEN A BATTLE? SOME CIVIL STRIFE?
THIS TOWN USED TO HAVE A LARGE TEMPLE, PRESIDED OVER BY A BRAHMIN HIGH PRIEST. IT WAS BUILT AND SUPPORTED THROUGH A DONATION FROM THE PLUTOCRAT VISAKHA.
SO LARGE WAS THE OFFERING THAT THE PRIESTS COULD DO AS THEY PLEASED AND LIVED IN GREAT LUXURY.

BUT A YEAR AGO, AN EPIDEMIC OF FEVER SWEPT THROUGH TOWN, CLAIMING MORE AND MORE LIVES EACH DAY...

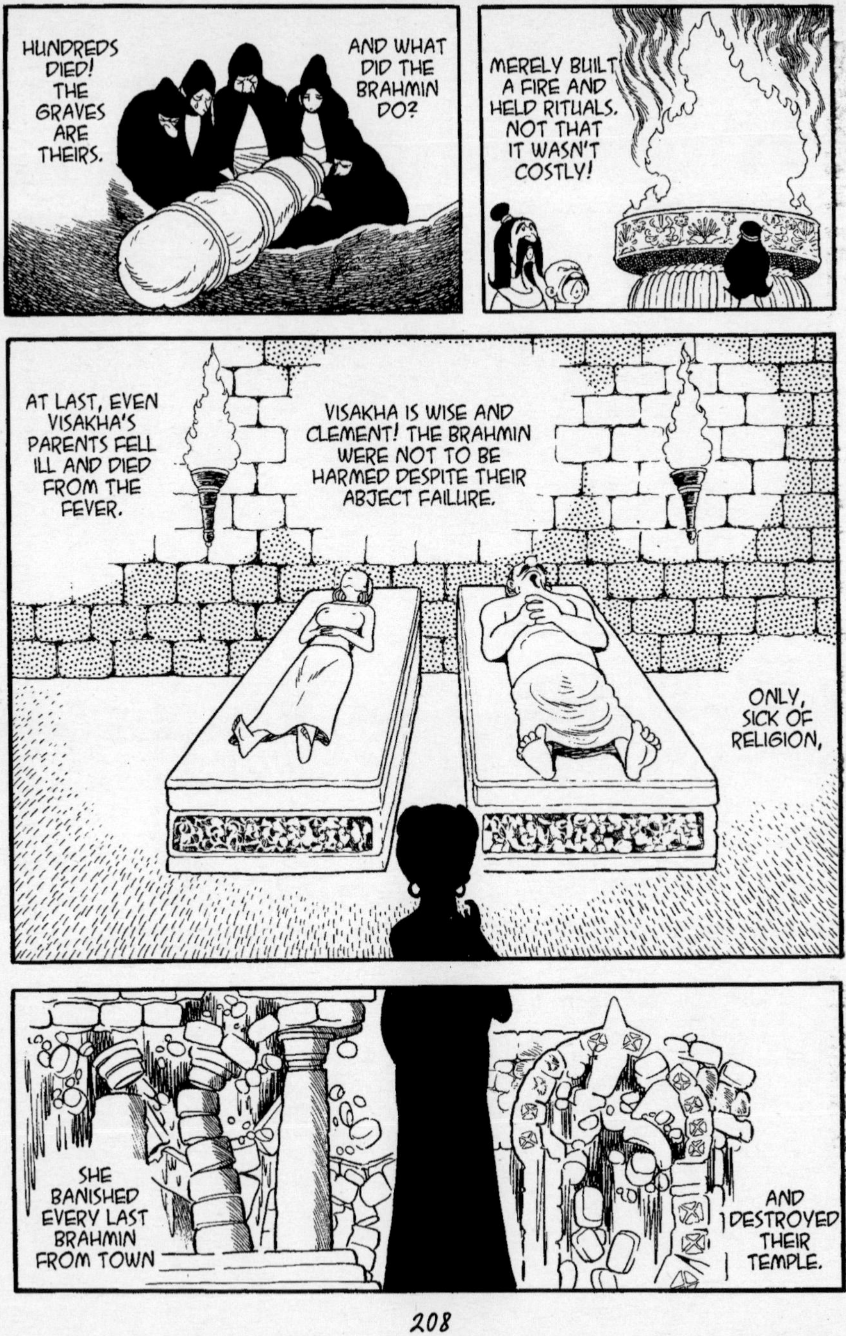

AT LAST, EVEN VISAKHA'S PARENTS FELL ILL AND DIED FROM THE FEVER.

VISAKHA IS WISE AND CLEMENT! THE BRAHMIN WERE NOT TO BE HARMED DESPITE THEIR ABJECT FAILURE.

ONLY, SICK OF RELIGION,

I SERVE HIS MAJESTY BIMBISARA OF MAGADHA! I AM THE KNIGHT SUKANDA!

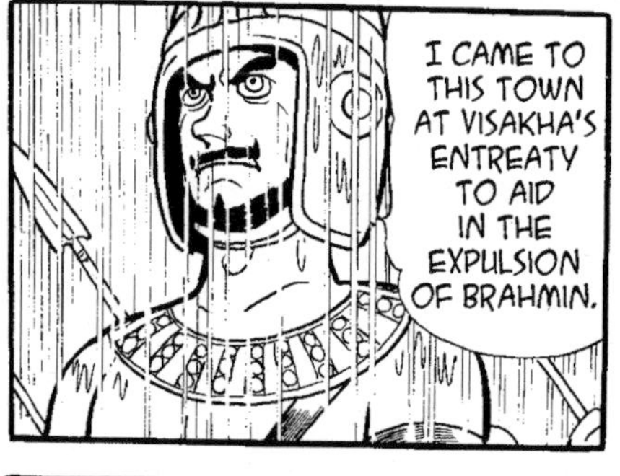
I CAME TO THIS TOWN AT VISAKHA'S ENTREATY TO AID IN THE EXPULSION OF BRAHMIN.

I UNDERSTAND. I AM DHEPA, MY FRIEND IS SIDDHARTHA.

WE HAVE NOTHING WHATSOEVER TO DO WITH THESE LOCAL BRAHMIN. AND WE ARE TRULY EXHAUSTED.
CAN WE NOT TAKE SHELTER, IF ONLY FOR THE DURATION OF THIS TORRENT?
WE WILL QUIT THE TOWN AS SOON AS THE SKY CLEARS.

HAH! AND LET THE BOY'S ILLNESS SPREAD...
SO THE STENCH OF DEATH MAY FILL THIS TOWN YET AGAIN?

SEIZE THE CHILD AND KILL HIM!

PERHAPS HIS FEVER IS NOT CONTA-GIOUS!
HE HAS CUT HIS LEG ON GRASS. LOOK! HIS WOUND IS FESTERING.
THE FEVER MAY BE FROM HIS WOUND!

HMM

GIVE US ONE DAY... NO, ONE NIGHT IS ALL I ASK.
LET ME NURSE THE BOY.

IF HIS FEVER DOES NOT BREAK BY DAWN, YOU MAY GO AHEAD AND KILL HIM.
YOU INTEND TO CURE HIM?
...IF YOU FAIL, WILL YOU DIE WITH HIM?

AS YOU WISH.

VERY WELL. WE'LL LET THEM STAY AMONG THE TEMPLE RUINS.

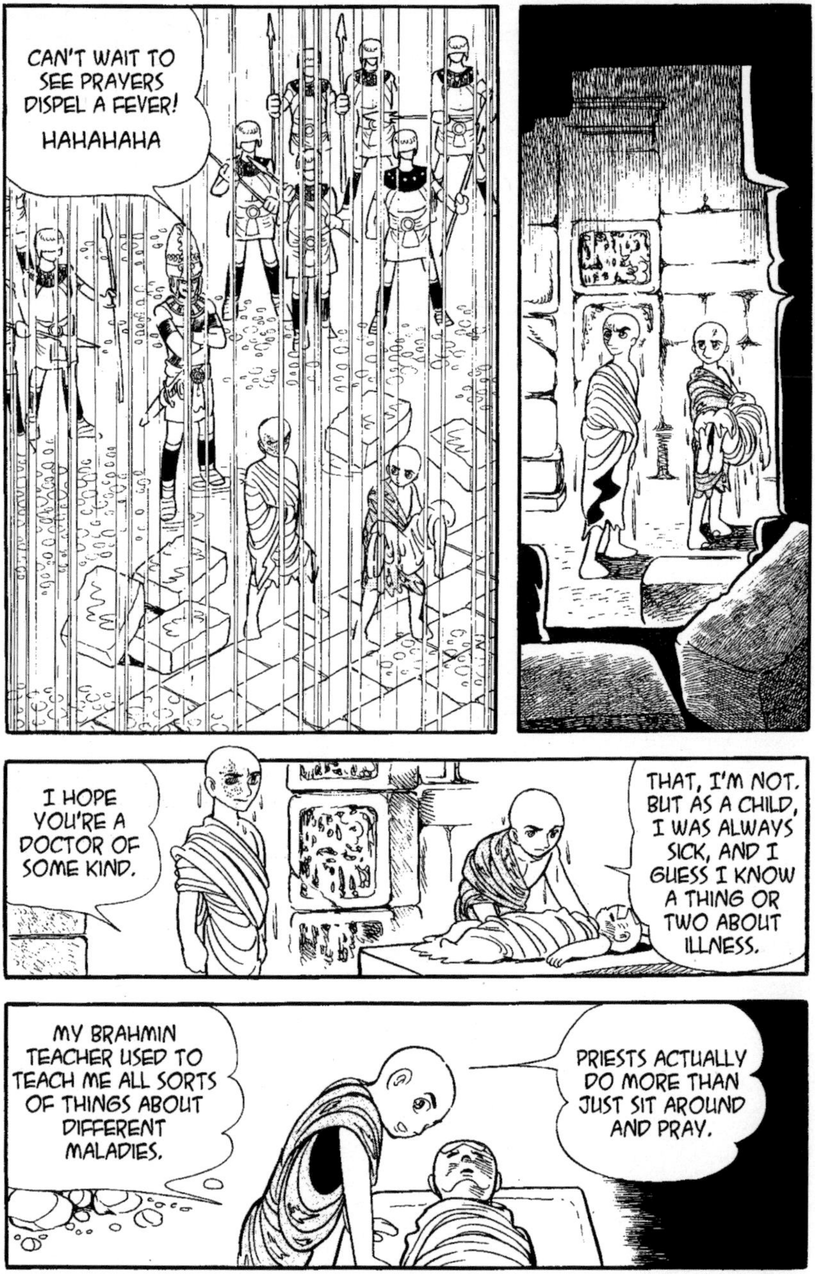

CAN'T WAIT TO SEE PRAYERS DISPEL A FEVER!
HAHAHAHA

I HOPE YOU'RE A DOCTOR OF SOME KIND.

THAT, I'M NOT. BUT AS A CHILD, I WAS ALWAYS SICK, AND I GUESS I KNOW A THING OR TWO ABOUT ILLNESS.

MY BRAHMIN TEACHER USED TO TEACH ME ALL SORTS OF THINGS ABOUT DIFFERENT MALADIES.

PRIESTS ACTUALLY DO MORE THAN JUST SIT AROUND AND PRAY.

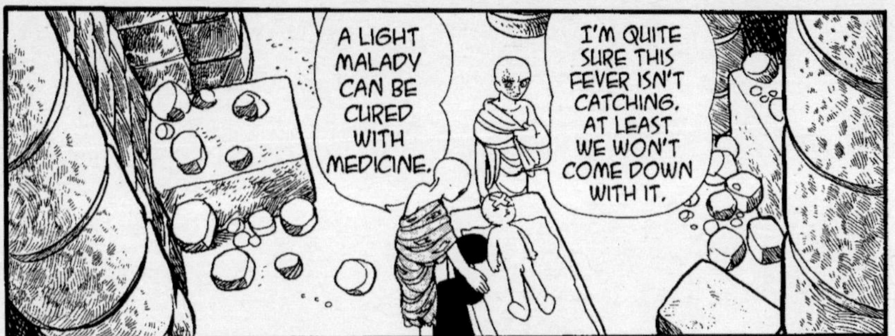
A LIGHT MALADY CAN BE CURED WITH MEDICINE.
I'M QUITE SURE THIS FEVER ISN'T CATCHING. AT LEAST WE WON'T COME DOWN WITH IT.

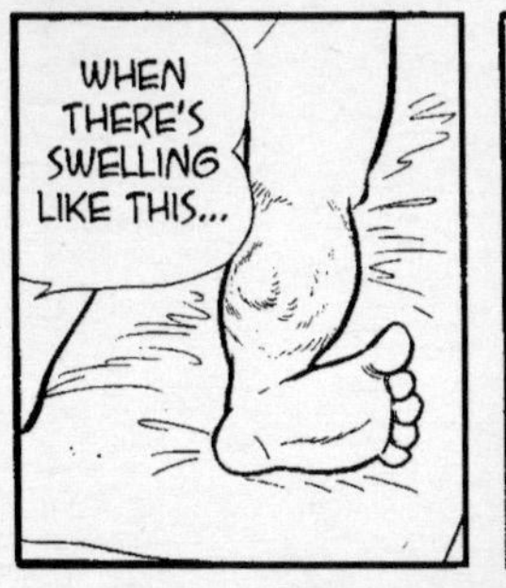
WHEN THERE'S SWELLING LIKE THIS...

THE PUS HAS TO BE DRAWN OUT, AND THE WOUND SEARED WITH HOT IRON. EATING BLUE MOLD HELPS, TOO.

DHEPA, COULD YOU GET A FIRE GOING AT THAT HEARTH?

YOU BETTER KNOW WHAT YOU'RE TALKING ABOUT. THAT GUY MEANT IT ABOUT KILLING YOU.

CAN YOU GET THOSE? I'LL COLLECT THE MOLD.
I NEED A BROKEN SPEAR, A LARGE POT, AND SOME CLOTHS.

SPLASH
SPLISH
SPLOSH
ANYONE HOME?
I NEED THE MOLD ON YOUR IRONWARE!
BET THEY WOULDN'T MIND...
...OF COURSE, HELP YOURSELF! I OUGHTA THANK YOU!

PLEASE SET THE WATER TO BOIL, AND THROW IN THE CLOTH.
AND HEAT THE SPEAR UNTIL IT GLOWS RED.
SIDDHARTHA, HOW ARE WE GOING TO DRAW OUT THE PUS? DON'T TELL ME...
SIDDHARTHA
SPIT

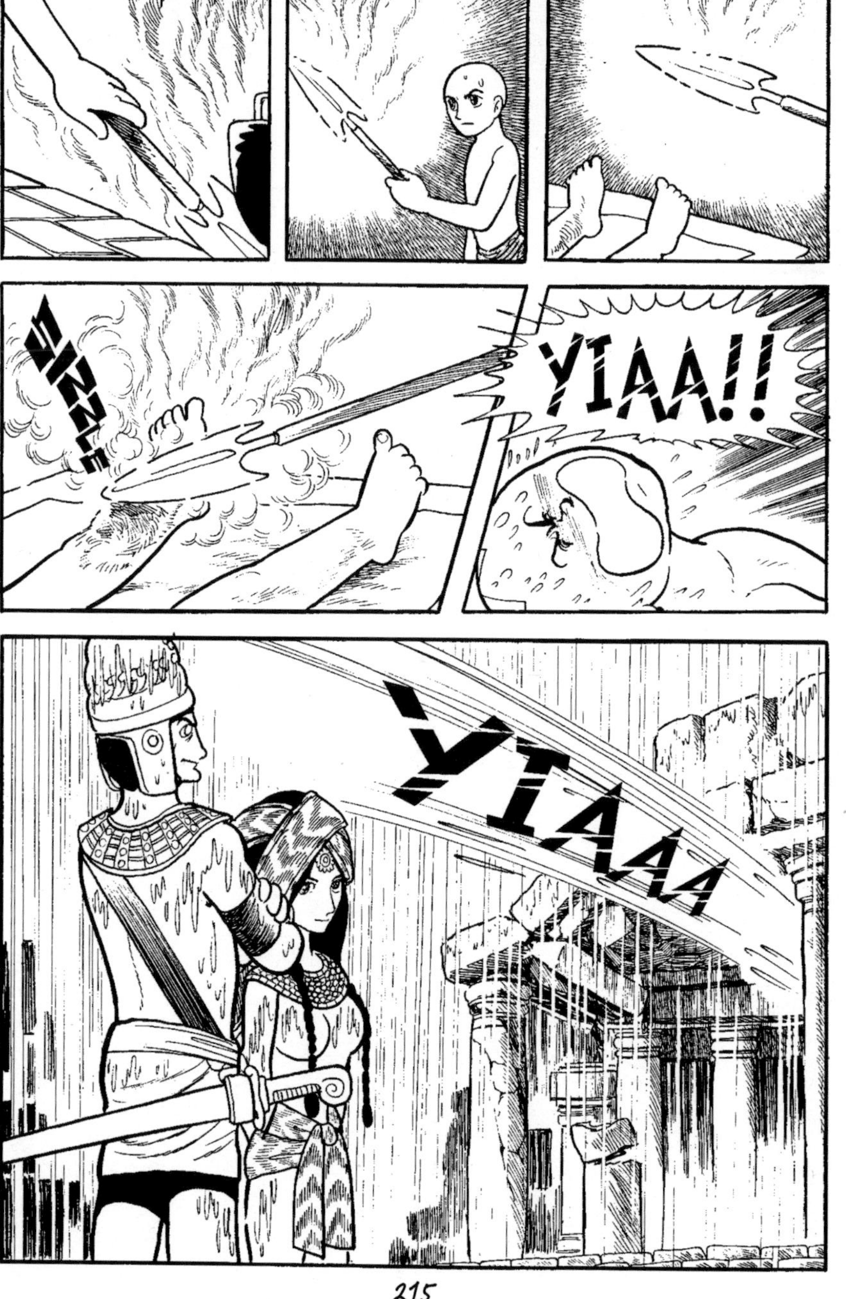
SIZZLE
YIAA!!
YIAAA

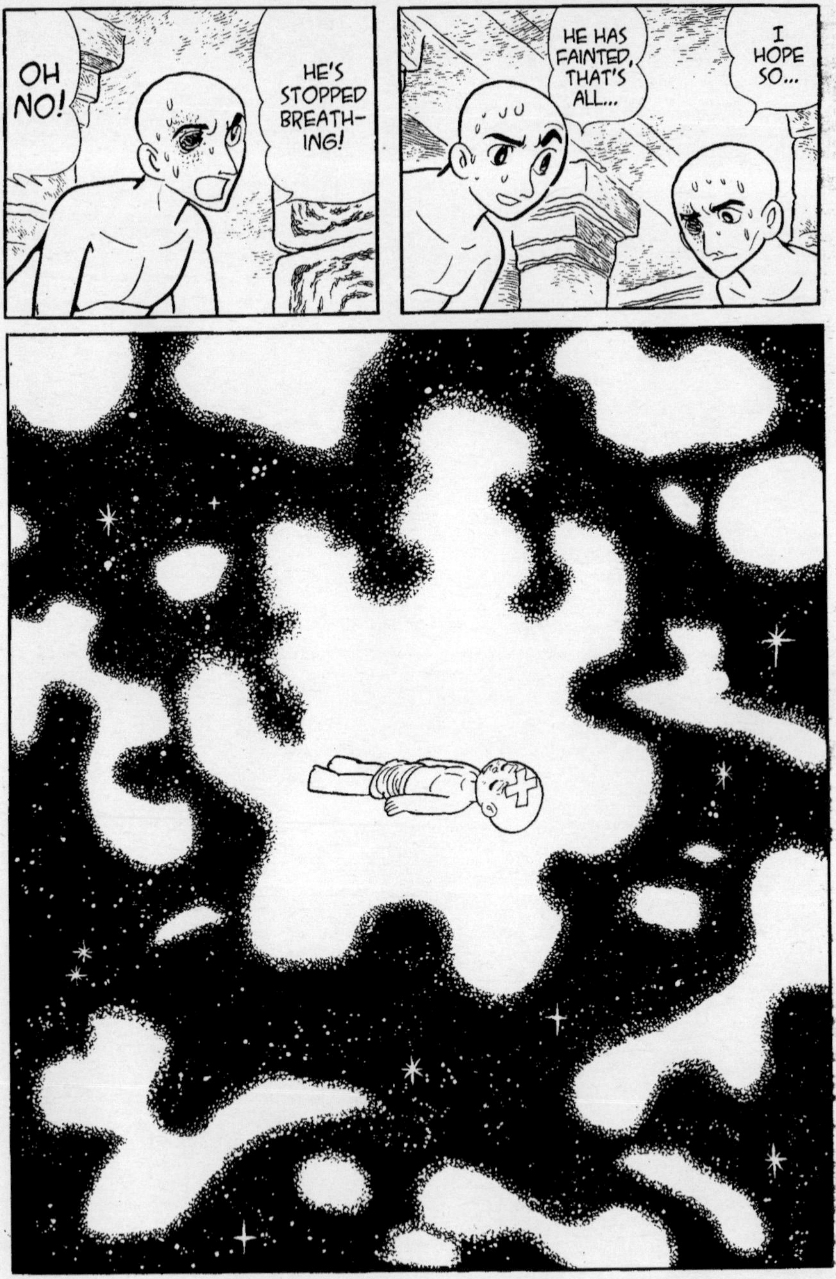

OH NO!
HE'S STOPPED BREATH-ING!

HE HAS FAINTED, THAT'S ALL...
I HOPE SO...

WHERE AM I? ME DEAD?
ASSAJI. YOU STAND ON THE THRESHOLD OF THE DOMAIN OF DEATH.
BUT YOU HAVEN'T COMPLETED THE LIFE BESTOWED UPON YOU. YOU MUST THEREFORE RETURN TO THE DOMAIN OF LIFE...
HOW MUCH MORE I LIVE?
TEN YEARS MORE. IN TEN YEARS, YOU MUST DIE. AS YOUR SIRE HAS SLAIN COUNTLESS BEASTS...
UNTIL THAT DAY, LIVE! WANDER THE EARTH FOR TEN YEARS TREMBLING IN FEAR OF YOUR FATED DEATH!
YOU IN TURN SHALL BE TORN APART BY BEASTS. THAT IS THE KARMIC LAW...

SIDDHARTHA, HE'S POURING SWEAT!
LET ME TRY THE TRICK WE USE
WHEN A MONK FAINTS DURING AN ORDEAL.
...YES! HE'S REVIVED, HE'S FAINTLY BREATHING!
HA
HA

HAA
HAA

THANK GOOD-NESS...

WE'VE SAVED HIM!
YESSS!! HA HA HA HA HA HA HA

SHHHH
SHHHH
SHHHH
SHHHH

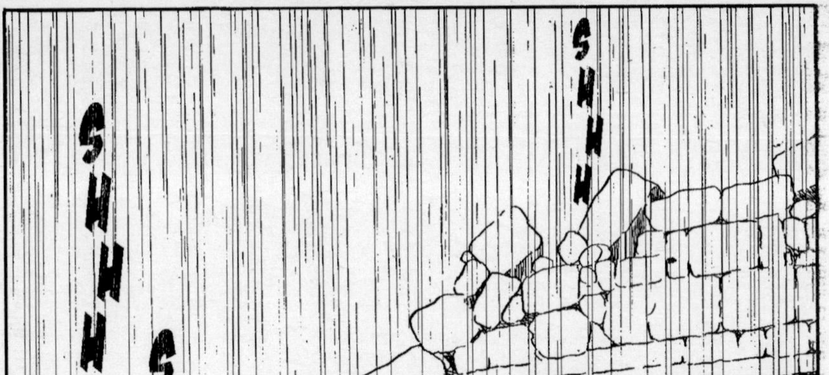

SHHH
SHHH
SHHH

DO YOU THINK THAT MONK SIDDHARTHA CAN CURE THE SICK?
SHHH
HE SEEMS TO THINK HE CAN.
SHHH

VISAKHA, YOU CANNOT STAND HERE ALL NIGHT IN THIS RAIN. YOU'LL FALL ILL!
OH? BUT I WORRY FOR THE YOUNG MONK. YOUR CONCERN IS UNWAR-RANTED.

YOU JEST !!
MY, HOW SCARY YOU LOOK.

SIR,

"SNICKER"
ARE YOU JEALOUS?

NONSENSE! WHY SHOULD I BE JEALOUS?
OR ENVIOUS?
OR FURIOUS?

PERHAPS THAT SIDDHARTHA IS OF ROYAL BLOOD.
THERE WAS A PRINCE IN KAPILAVASTU BY THAT NAME.

IF HE IS A PRINCE, HOW INTRIGUING.
I'D LIKE TO HEAR HIS STORY.

I WILL NOT STAND FOR THIS FOOLISHNESS! DO NOT FORGET THAT YOU ARE BETROTHED TO ME!
SEE. YOU ARE JEALOUS, AFTER ALL.

VISAKHA!!

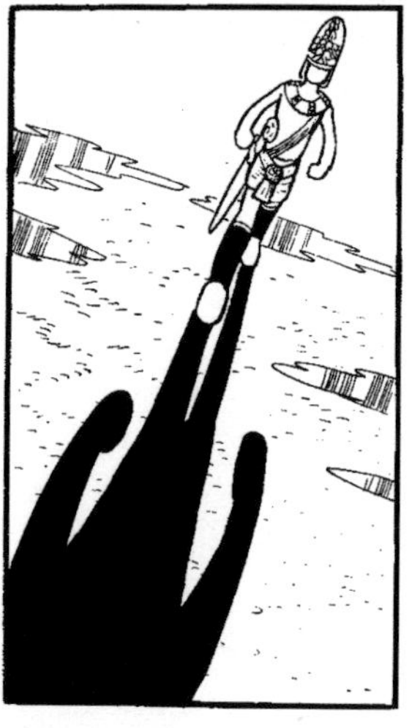

DAY HAS BROKEN, SIDDHARTHA. STEP FORTH!

THE BOY!
HE'S CURED?
YES, HE SWEATED BUCKETS, AND THE FEVER SUBSIDED.
snif
IT WASN'T THE CONTAGIOUS KIND.
SO ARE WE REPRIEVED, SIR KNIGHT?
YOU WON'T BE EXECUTED... BUT I CANNOT ALLOW YOU TO STAY IN THIS TOWN.
YOU PROMISED TO QUIT TOWN WHEN THE SKY CLEARED. THE SKY IS CLEAR! NOW TAKE YOUR LEAVE.

WHAT ARE YOU WAITING FOR? I SAID GO!
BUT WE BARELY SLEPT LAST NIGHT! GIVE US SOME TIME TO REST!
WHY DRIVE THEM AWAY LIKE THAT, SUKANDA?
B-BUT VISAKHA...
TRAVELERS, I WELCOME YOU ALL TO MY MANSION. HOW ABOUT SOME BREAKFAST?
YOU ARE VERY KIND.

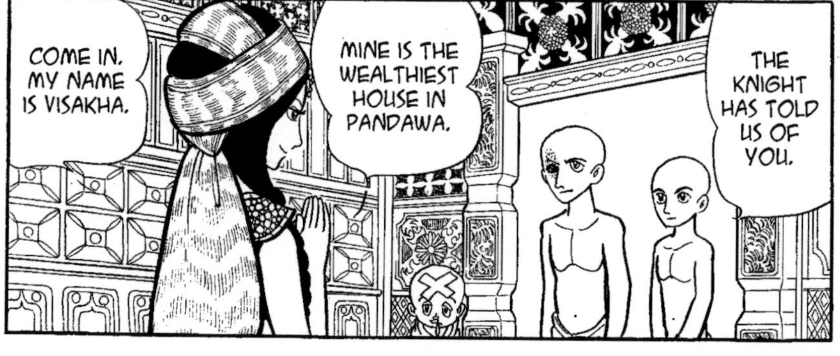

WE ARE MOST PROVINCIAL HERE; I AM EAGER TO HEAR TALES OF OTHER LANDS.
YA WOW !

CHOMP
SLURP
CHOMP
GOBBLE

CRUNCH
GNAW
CHEW

HAVE YOU EVER? THE JAWS OF DEATH MUST GIVE ONE AN APPETITE.

MUNCH
MUNCH
MUNCH
MUNCH

MUSH
MUSH

GULP
GULP
GULP

MMMM

GOBBLE
MUNCH
CRUNCH

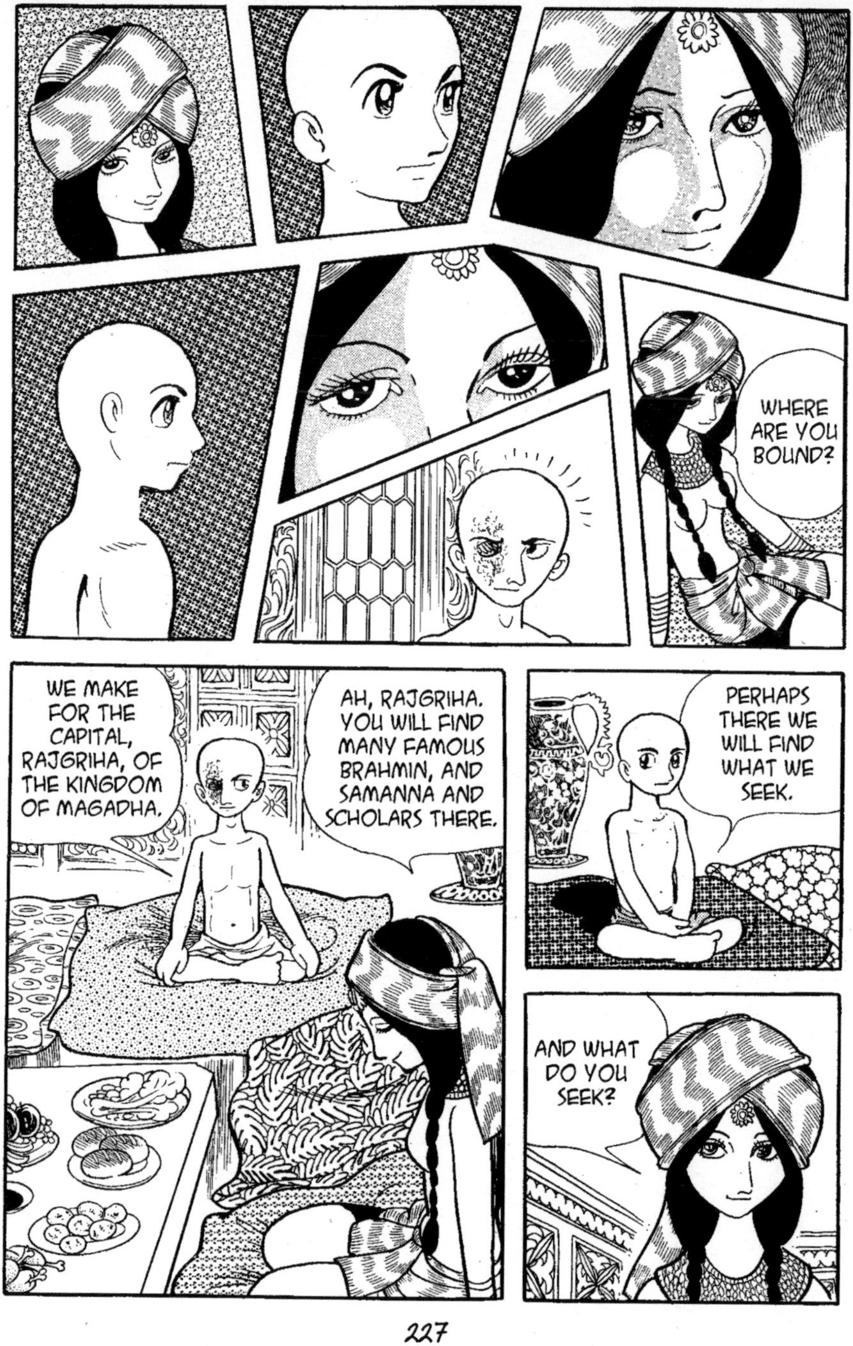

WHERE ARE YOU BOUND?

Hahahaha
Oh
Haha
Hohoho
Ahah
Haha

IF THERE WERE SUCH A THING, I WOULD BUY IT...
COME, I HAVE SOMETHING TO SHOW YOU.
CREAK
WHAT ARE THESE ?
POTIONS. I BOUGHT THEM ALL UP FROM A MERCHANT WHO CAME FROM THE FAR WEST.

THESE POTIONS WORK MAGIC.

THAT ONE TURNS YOU INTO A BIRD.
I DON'T BELIEVE YOU !

YET I HAVE FLOWN THE SKIES AS A BIRD! AND NOT JUST ONCE!
I DON'T BELIEVE YOU.
SURELY IT ONLY MAKES YOU FEEL THAT WAY?

THIS ONE IS A YOUTH POTION.
IT TURNS YOU INTO A CHILD, FOR A DAY.

SMASH
HA HA HA HA

THESE ARE MERE DRUGS.
YES, I KNOW. BUT LIFE IS SO CRUELLY SHORT.
HOW ELSE AM I TO COPE WITH THAT?

VISAKHA, I HAVE BUSINESS IN MAGADHA. FARE WELL WHILE I AM GONE.
SAMANNA, PREPARE TO DEPART! I CAN GUIDE YOU TO THE KINGDOM IF YOU WISH.

WHY ALL THE RUSH?
THE MONKS HAVE NO REASON TO DALLY.
THE TROOPS ARE LINED UP AND READY TO GO.

THEN A FAREWELL TOAST.

I DO NOT DRINK!
HOW VERY UPRIGHT! IT'S JUST FRUIT WINE!

MARCH!
LEFT
LEFT

WHAT IS IT WITH THE SACK?
LEFT
sniffle

LEFTOVERS. LUNCH FOR A WEEK.
RIGHT

LEFT!

STOMP
STOMP
STOMP
STOMP

STOMP
STOMP

...

OH, DEAR... I'M SUDDENLY... SO... SLEEPY... YAWWWN
NO WONDER. SO MUCH FOOD, AFTER HARDLY A WINK LAST NIGHT.
CAN'T TAKE ANOTHER STEP. PLEASE GO ON AHEAD!
FINE, SEE YOU LATER.
MUMBLE MUMBLE
S T O M P
S T O M P
S T O M P
S T O M P
WELL DONE.

HUNH? WHERE...
WHERE AM I?!

FEAR NOT. I HAD YOU BROUGHT HERE AFTER YOUR COLLAPSE.
WHERE ARE THE OTHERS? WHERE'S DHEPA?
I'VE NO IDEA. MAYBE THEY WENT ON AHEAD?
ACTUALLY, JUST NOW, SOME TROOPS CAME BACK LOOKING FOR YOU. I TOLD THEM YOU WEREN'T HERE.
WHY?
I'VE GOTTA GO...
ACH... MY HEAD'S SPINNING.
YOU NEED TO TAKE THIS ANTIDOTE.
ARE YOU TELLING ME...
I'VE BEEN DRUGGED?
chuckle
JUST A MILD SEDATIVE.
DON'T GO!! SIDDHARTHA, YOU CAN'T!

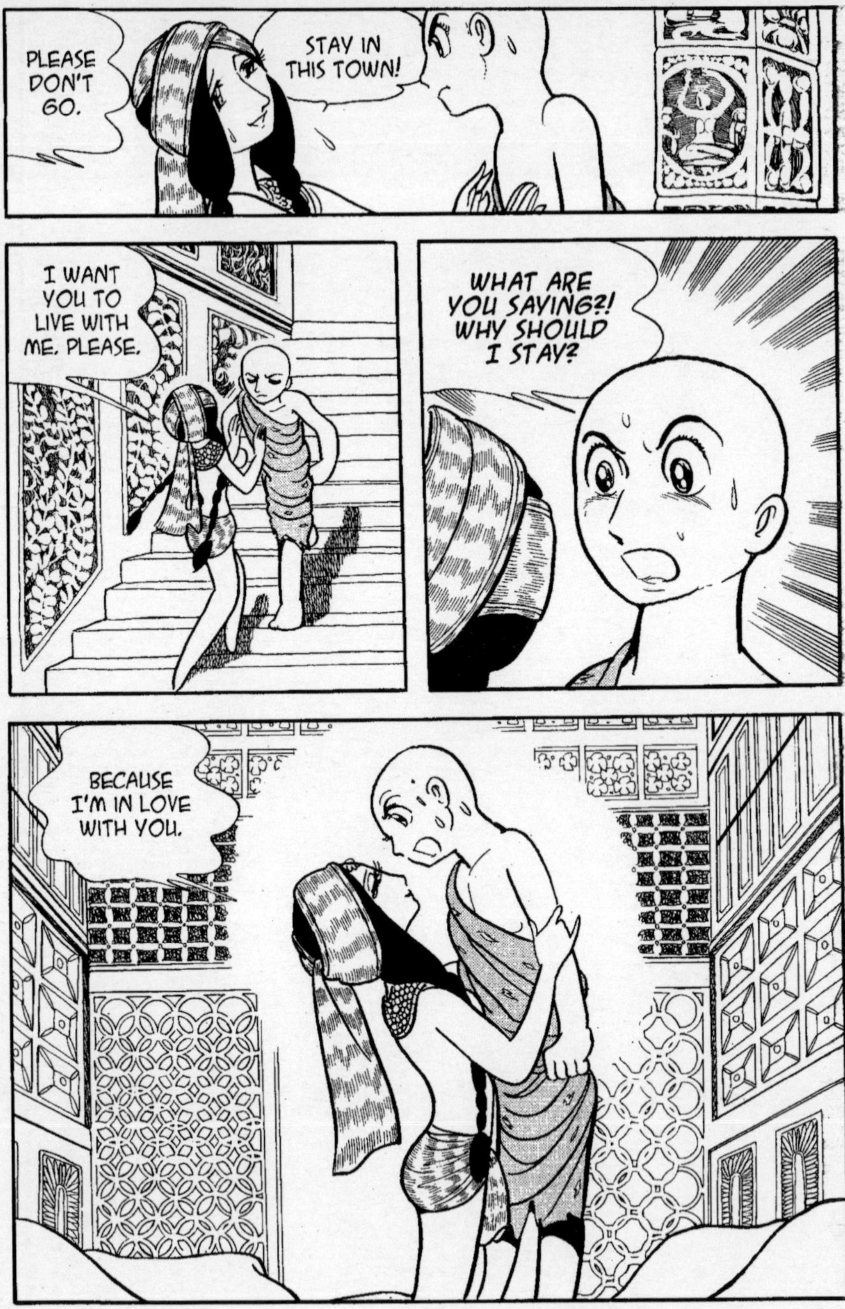

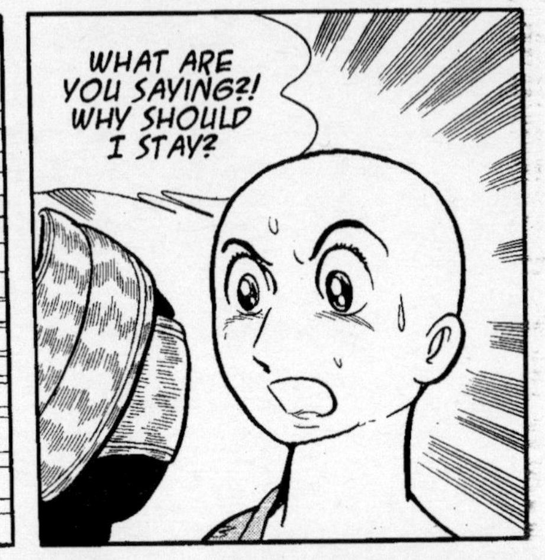

BECAUSE I'M IN LOVE WITH YOU.

I KNOW THAT I'M ENGAGED TO SUKANDA...
BUT I CAN'T HELP MYSELF.
I'VE FALLEN IN LOVE WITH YOU...
GI-GI-GIVE ME A BREAK!
SIDDHARTHA, PRINCE OF KAPILAVASTU, HEIR TO KING SUDDHODANA AND THE SHAKYA THRONE...
AND YET, YOU FASCINATE ME NOT ON ACCOUNT OF YOUR LINEAGE...
BUT AS A MAN WHO HAS COME INTO MY LIFE...
THAT'S ENOUGH!
LISTEN, VISAKHA! I HAVE BOTH QUEEN AND CHILD BACK IN KAPILAVASTU. I ABANDONED THEM JUST SO I COULD PURSUE THIS PATH AND WEATHER HARDSHIPS.
I AM DEVOTED TO THIS LIFE, TO THE EXCLUSION OF ALL ELSE!

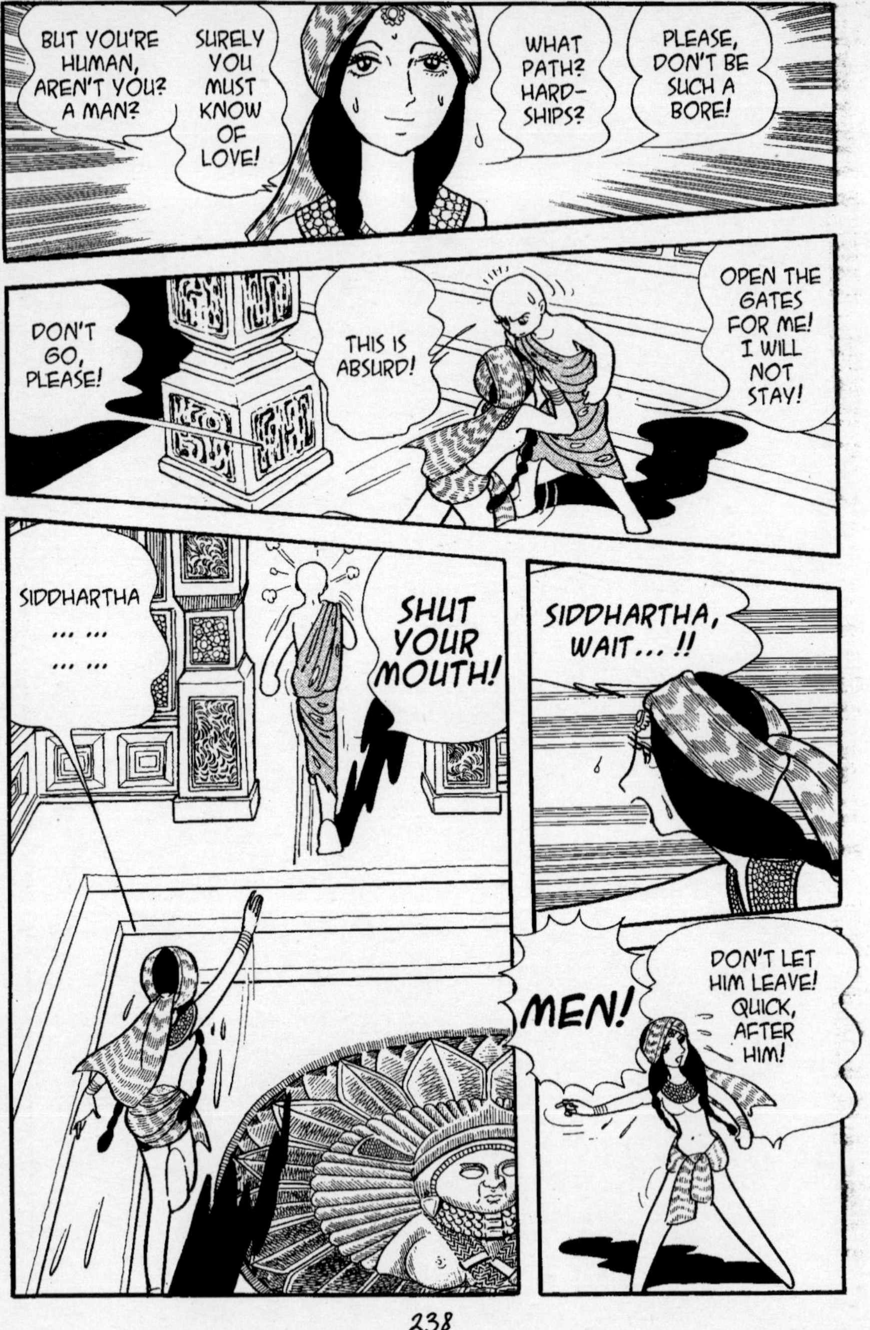

BUT YOU'RE HUMAN, AREN'T YOU? A MAN?
SURELY YOU MUST KNOW OF LOVE!
WHAT PATH? HARD-SHIPS?
PLEASE, DON'T BE SUCH A BORE!
DON'T GO, PLEASE!
THIS IS ABSURD!
OPEN THE GATES FOR ME! I WILL NOT STAY!
SIDDHARTHA ... ...
SHUT YOUR MOUTH!
SIDDHARTHA, WAIT... !!
MEN!
DON'T LET HIM LEAVE! QUICK, AFTER HIM!

HEH HEH
SIR MONK

EXCUSE US, BUT THE MISTRESS WANTS YOU.

AYY
UGH

HEY YA FOLKS IN THERE, OPEN WIDE YER GATES! WE'RE A HUMBLE GANG LOOKIN' TO DO SOME WORK IN YOUR TOWN! HOPE YOU LIKED OUR INTRODUCTION!
Roar
Guffaw
cheer
Hehehehe
Hahaha

Hehehehe
Hahaha
Hahaha
Hahaha
Hehehehe
Hahaha

THAT'S...!

MY LADY!

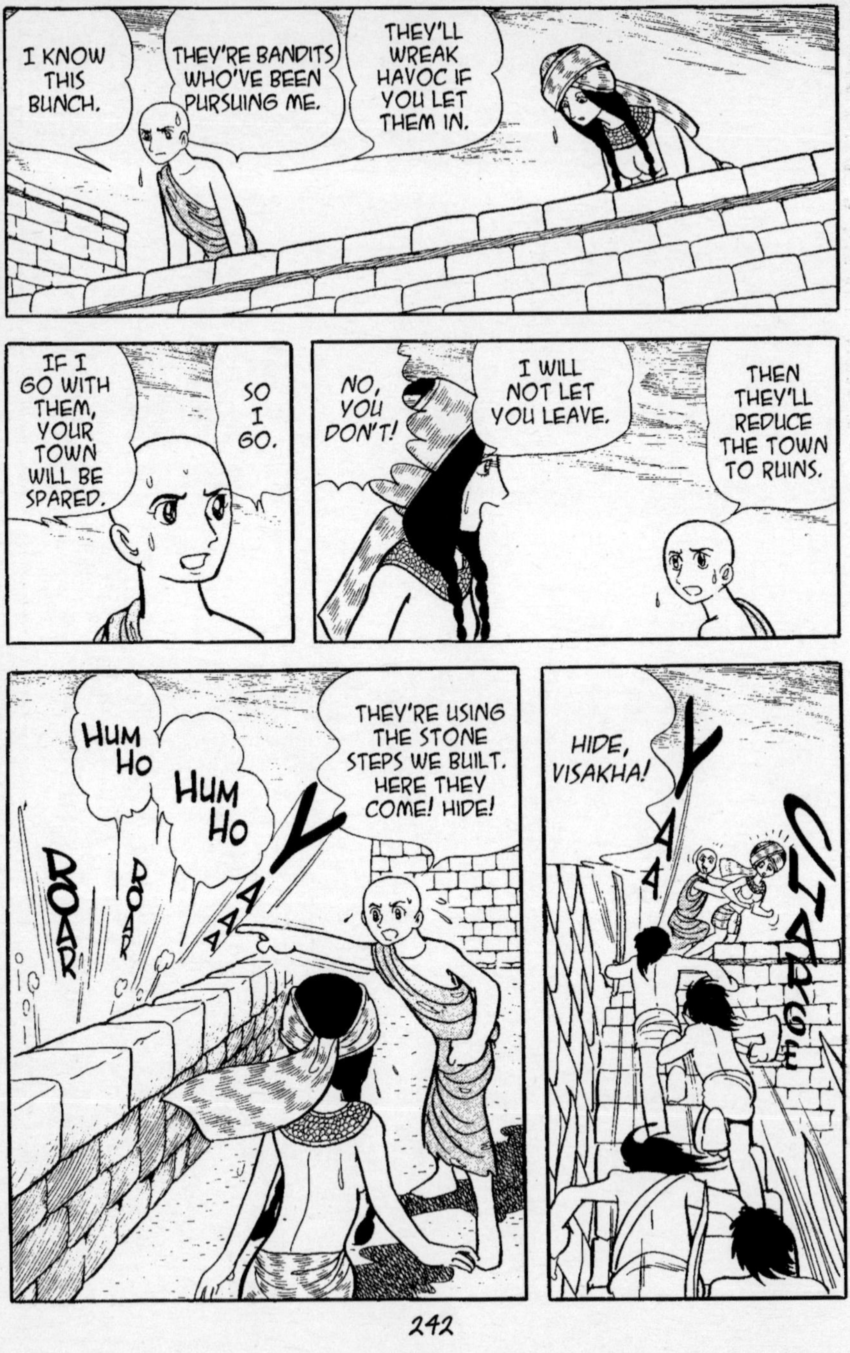

I KNOW THIS BUNCH.
THEY'RE BANDITS WHO'VE BEEN PURSUING ME.
THEY'LL WREAK HAVOC IF YOU LET THEM IN.

IF I GO WITH THEM, YOUR TOWN WILL BE SPARED.
SO I GO.
NO, YOU DON'T!
I WILL NOT LET YOU LEAVE.
THEN THEY'LL REDUCE THE TOWN TO RUINS.

HUM HO
HUM HO
ROAR
ROAR
THEY'RE USING THE STONE STEPS WE BUILT. HERE THEY COME! HIDE!
YAAAA
HIDE, VISAKHA!
YAA
CHARGE

AH, SIDDHARTHA, SO WE MEET AGAIN! I HAD A HUNCH YOU MIGHT BE HERE.
WHO'S THE DAME?! I CAN SMELL HER PERFUME.

VISAKHA, A NOTABLE OF THIS TOWN...
YOU MUST NOT HARM HER! NOR THE TOWN! IN RETURN, I WILL COME WITH YOU.

AH HA... PROTECTING THIS TOWN, ARE WE? A FINE PLACE IT MUST BE!
IT'D BE A SHAME TO JUST GO OFF WITH YOU AND NOT EXPLORE IT SOME.

MEN, HAVE A LOOK AROUND. OH, AND HELP YOURSELF TO ANYTHING SHINY. CALL IT A SOUVENIR!
AYE!
MERCY!

TATTA, CALL THEM OFF, I BEG YOU FOR OLD TIMES' SAKE! I THOUGHT WE WERE FRIENDS!
HA, THAT'S RICH! CLAIMING FRIENDSHIP WHEN IT SUITS YOU. NOT THAT I MIND, BUT I'VE GOT A BUSINESS TO RUN.
WHEE, LOOK AT ALL THE STUFF! GRAB EVERYTHING IN SIGHT!
AIEE!
SHUT YER TRAP.
MURDER
MAY I COME IN ?
AAAH!
HELP!!

STOP! TAKE WHAT YOU WANT, BUT DON'T RUIN OUR TOWN!!
I'M SORRY, MISS. MY MEN JUST DON'T KNOW THEIR MANNERS, DO THEY?
oh!
GUESSING FROM YOUR VOICE, I BET YOURS IS A PRETTY FACE! MIND IF I MARKED IT SOME?
M-I-G-A-I-L-A
WHAT'S SHE DONE TO YOU?!
HEH HEH, NOW WAIT A SEC. ARE SHE AND YOU LOVERS, SIDDHARTHA? IS THAT IT?
MISS, THERE WAS A TIME WHEN I WENT HEAD OVER HEELS FOR THIS HERE BEAU... AND LOOK WHAT I GOT FOR MY TENDER FEELINGS.
THIS FACE! TAKE A GOOD LOOK!
LOVE CAN MAKE YOU BLIND!
HA HA HA HA

I DON'T ACCEPT ADVICE FROM SHUDRA!
BACK OFF, YOU SLAVE!

WHAT ?!
...YOU BITCH !!

DAAAAH

ARE YOU CRAZY?
LADY VISA-KHA !!
THANK GOODNESS SHE FELL ON SOFT SAND.

BOSS, WE GOT EVERYTHING WORTH TAKING.
WHAT'S THE PLAN FOR THE REST?
HMM, HOW 'BOUT SOME FIREWORKS?
STOP THIS!
HOW CRUEL CAN YOU BE?!

FLARE

TATTA, I'VE HAD IT WITH YOU! THIS IS REALLY IT BETWEEN YOU AND ME.
DON'T BE SOUR, CHIEF.
NOW GET LOST.
C'EST LA VIE, NON?

GUYS, LET'S CLEAR OUT!

SHE'LL BE A NUISANCE, SIDDHARTHA. DUMP HER!
SHUSH. HE LIKES HANGING OUT WITH HER, OBVIOUSLY. LET HIM DO AS HE WANTS.
DO NOT DESPAIR, VISAKHA!
SNIFF *SOB* *GROAN*

RISE AND SHINE... HA HA HA
TATTA !!

WHERE ARE WE?

INSIDE MOUNT PANDAVA, ON THE MAGADHA BORDER.

HOW COULD YOU SET FIRE TO THAT TOWN? YOU BEAST! YOU'LL NEVER GET AWAY WITH IT!
AND WHERE'S VISAKHA? IF YOU'VE DONE ANYTHING HORRIBLE TO HER —

CALM DOWN. SHE'S A VALUABLE HOSTAGE. THE LADS ARE LOOKING AFTER HER.
WHERE IS SHE?

RELAX, RELAX!

SIDDHARTHA, I WANNA HAVE A SERIOUS TALK WITH YOU, MAN TO MAN.
WE DON'T GET THE CHANCE EVERY DAY.

I HATE TO DISAPPOINT YOU, BUT I'M A MONK AND YOU'RE A BANDIT. WE'VE NOTHING TO DISCUSS!

DON'T BE LIKE THAT.
WE USED TO BE FRIENDS ONCE.

SIDDHARTHA... WHY DO YOU HAVE TO BE SO STUBBORN ANYWAY?

WHAT CAN I DO TO MAKE YOU DROP THIS WHOLE MONK THING?
THAT, AGAIN? WHETHER OR NOT I CONTINUE AS A MONK IS NONE OF YOUR BUSINESS.

WHAT, YOU WANT ME TO ABANDON MY ROBES SO THAT I CAN WAGE WAR ON KOSALA?
THEN YOU CAN CRUSH KOSALA!
I WANT YOU TO BE KING OF THE SHAKYA!
SORRY, BUT I HATE WAR!
BUT THAT'S WHERE YOU'RE WRONG! IT IS MY BUSINESS! WHAT I WOULDN'T GIVE FOR YOU TO QUIT!
THEN THE SHAKYA ARE SUNK.
LISTEN. FOR THE SAKE OF PURSUING THIS PATH...
I CAST AWAY BOTH FAMILY AND COUNTRY. I CAN'T JUST —

YOU'LL REALLY... RETURN ALL THE...?
...
OKAY, OKAY! THEN HOW 'BOUT A DEAL: IF YOU COME BACK, I'LL GIVE UP THIEVIN'.
I'LL DISBAND THE GANG, GIVE BACK ALL THE LOOT, AND LET THE HOSTAGE GO.
DON'T DO THIS TO ME!!
YEAH. AND I'LL DO ANYTHING ELSE YOU ASK ME TO DO. WANNA SEE ME POKE OUT MY EYE?
JUST LET VISAKHA GO... PLEASE.
Scritch
MAN, YOU'RE A HANDFUL... LIKE YOU'VE ALWAYS BEEN... ANYWAY, I'M GIVING YOU MY WORD!
JUST GIVE IT SOME THOUGHT, WILL YA?
I KNOW YOU'LL COME AROUND!

SOLDIERS, BOSS! HEADED THIS WAY!
MAGADHAN REGULARS!
WHAT
MAYBE THEY KNOW WHAT WE DONE TO THE TOWN!
THEY'RE AFTER US!!
SHEE-IT! SNIFFED US OUT LIKE DOGS! THAT'S NO PICNIC THEY'RE ON.
SO BE IT. WE'LL USE THE HOSTAGE AS A SHIELD AND FIGHT 'EM.

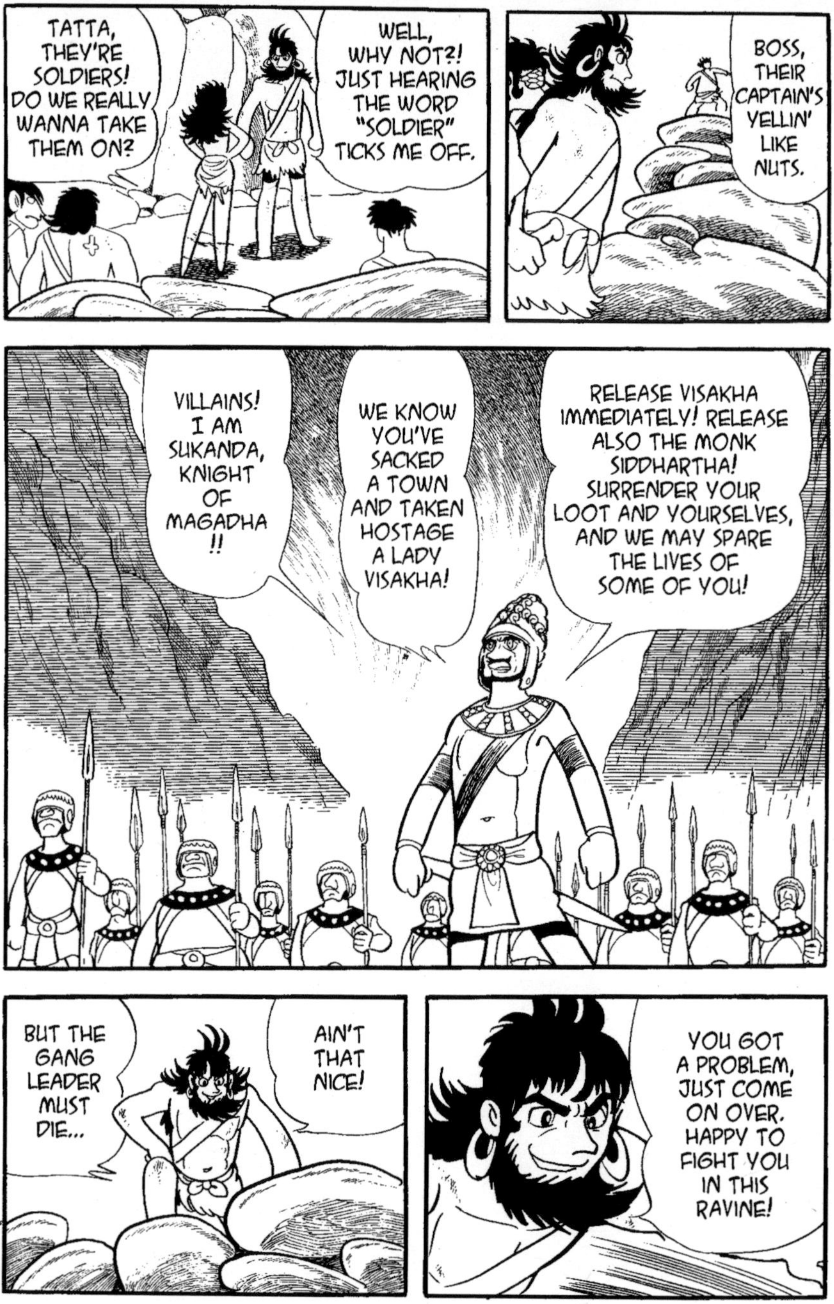

VILLAINS! I AM SUKANDA, KNIGHT OF MAGADHA !!

WE KNOW YOU'VE SACKED A TOWN AND TAKEN HOSTAGE A LADY VISAKHA!

RELEASE VISAKHA IMMEDIATELY! RELEASE ALSO THE MONK SIDDHARTHA! SURRENDER YOUR LOOT AND YOURSELVES, AND WE MAY SPARE THE LIVES OF SOME OF YOU!

DAMN BANDITS WOULDN'T BE HALF AS BOLD IF THEY DIDN'T HAVE HOSTAGES!
CAPTAIN! I SAY WE CHARGE INTO THE RAVINE AND WIPE OUT THOSE VERMIN!
WE'D BE PLAYING RIGHT INTO THEIR HANDS.

BESIDES, I WORRY FOR THE LADY'S SAFETY.
TAKE UP POSITIONS AT THE MOUTH OF THE RAVINE. I WILL GO ALONE.

ARE YOU SERIOUS?
I'LL SCALE THE SLOPE AND SNEAK INTO THEIR CAMP.

I'LL FIND THEIR LEADER, DESTROY HIM, AND RESCUE THE LADY VISAKHA.
I LEAVE YOU IN CHARGE.

GOOD LUCK, CAPT'N!

PSST, IT'S ME! OH, VISAKHA, POOR THING! YOU'RE OK NOW.

SHHHH

WHAT A SURPRISE, CAPTAIN.

SNUCK UP HERE LIKE A WEASEL!
MAN, YOU'RE THE REAL THING, COME TO SAVE YOUR DAMSEL...
WHOOM!

CLANG
SCOUNDREL

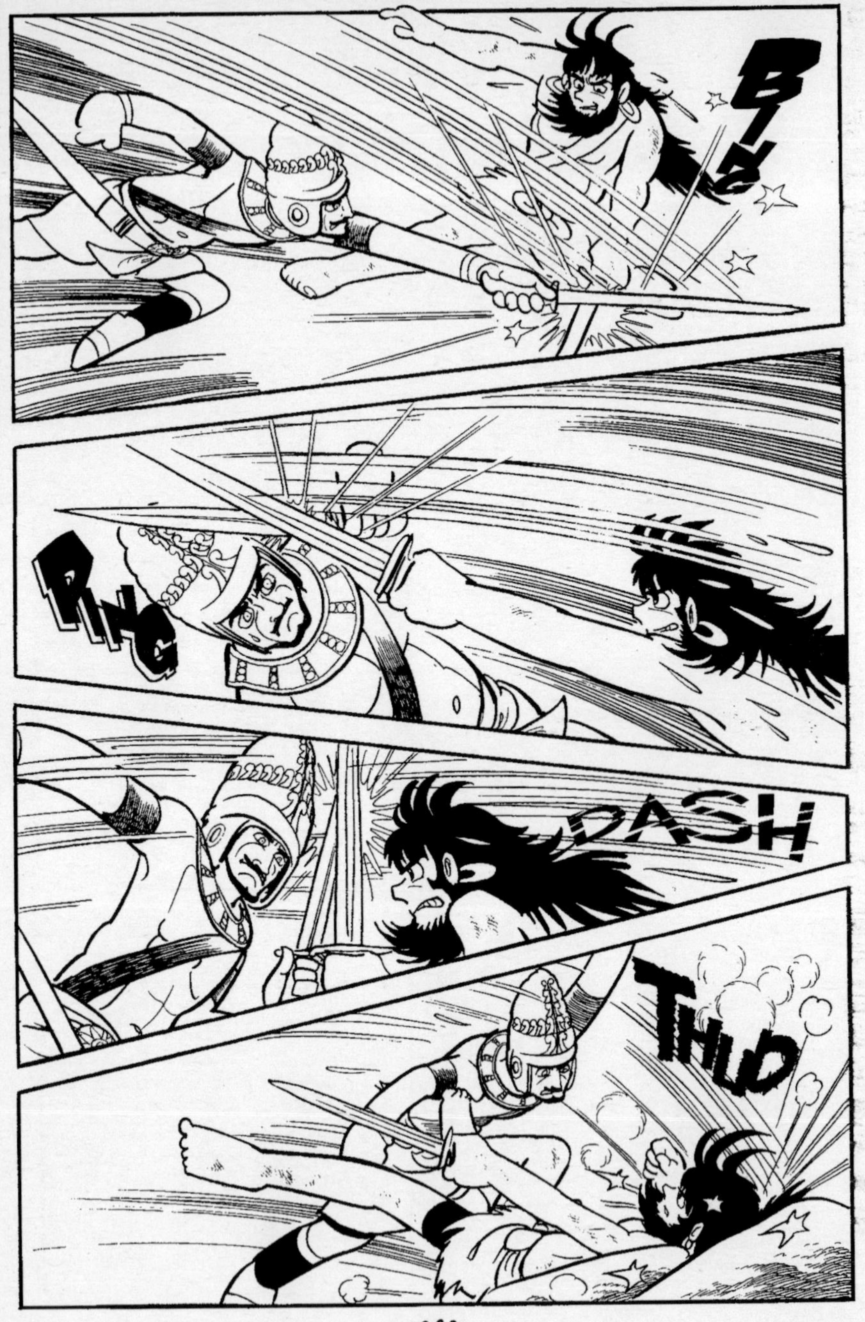
BING
RING
DASH
THUD

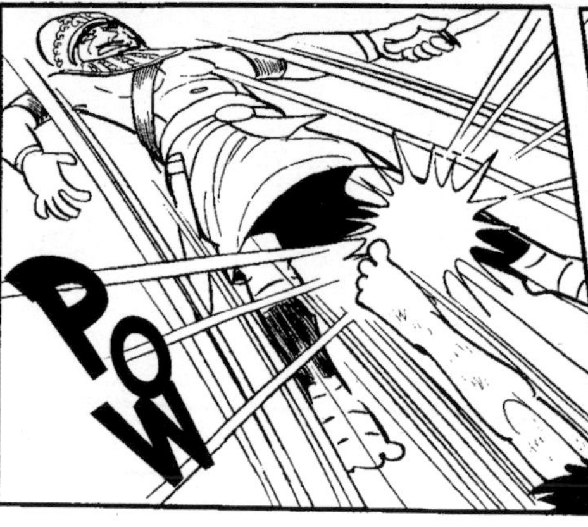
POW

ARRR

CLANK

GASH

PANT
PANT
PUFF
PANT

PANT
PANT
DIE!!
PANT
PANT
STOP!!

OUT OF THE WAY, MONK. OR DO YOU WANT TO DIE WITH HIM?
STOP THIS
STAY OUT OF THIS.
ONE OF US HAS TO DIE.

NEITHER, I SAY.
LAY DOWN YOUR SWORDS. OR FACE ME.

PERFECT! THAT STUPID FACE OF YOURS TURNS MY STOMACH!

WHANNNG

I DON'T BELIEVE IT...

YOU STOPPED MY SWORD... MONK, WHERE DID YOU LEARN TO FIGHT?

AH, YES. YOU'RE KSHATRIYA. ONCE A WARRIOR, HUH?
'TIS A FAIR FIGHT THEN!
WHO CARES WHAT I WAS? I DON'T WANT TO FIGHT. I SAID STOP!

TATTA, I'VE MADE UP MY MIND. I'M GOING BACK TO MY COUNTRY.
WHAT DID YOU JUST SAY?

TEN YEARS.
IN TEN YEARS, I'LL GO HOME.

TO KAPILA-VASTU?
YOU REALLY MEAN IT?

IN TURN YOU MUST DO AS YOU PROMISED. RELEASE VISAKHA AT ONCE, AND FORSWEAR BANDITRY.

SURE!
NOT A PROBLEM.

HA HA! YOU'VE MADE MY DAY!
WHAT'S TEN YEARS? I CAN WAIT!

YOU HEARD, SUKANDA.
YOU CAME FOR VISAKHA, RIGHT? THE BANDIT JUST RELEASED HER.

... ...
ROTTEN BASTARDS! FILTHY MAGGOTS!

A PLAGUE ON ME IF I DON'T CHOP HIS HEAD OFF IN THE KING'S VIEW!

CALM DOWN! HE'S AGREED TO GIVE UP BANDITRY AND REFORM.
SHUT UP!!

I HAVE NO TIME FOR YOUR STORIES! YOU, WHO SNUCK BACK INTO TOWN TO SEDUCE MY INTENDED! I'LL HAVE YOU FRAMED, AND EXECUTED WITH HIM!

YOU'RE WRONG!

IT WAS I WHO TRIED TO SEDUCE HIM.

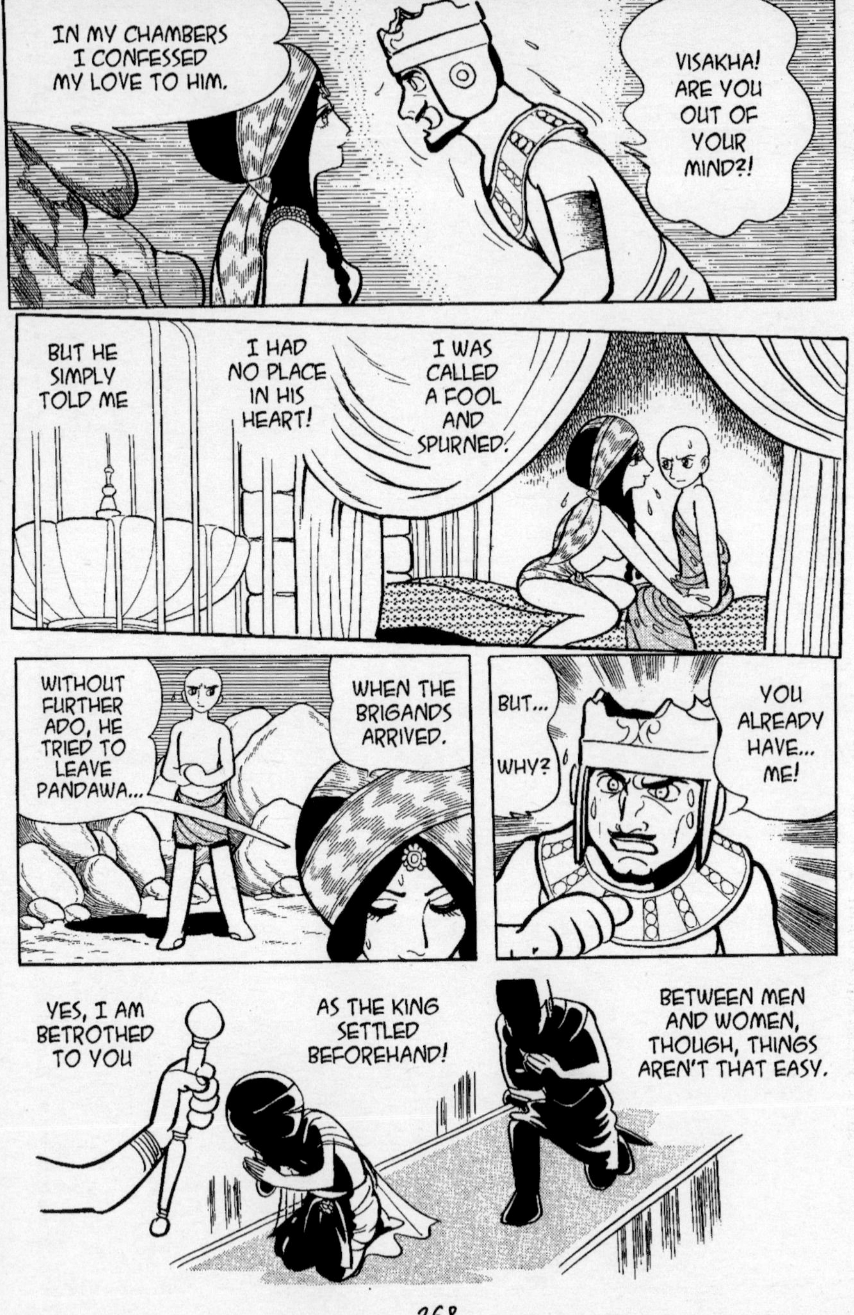
IN MY CHAMBERS I CONFESSED MY LOVE TO HIM.
VISAKHA! ARE YOU OUT OF YOUR MIND?!
BUT HE SIMPLY TOLD ME
I HAD NO PLACE IN HIS HEART!
I WAS CALLED A FOOL AND SPURNED.
WITHOUT FURTHER ADO, HE TRIED TO LEAVE PANDAWA...
WHEN THE BRIGANDS ARRIVED.
BUT...
WHY?
YOU ALREADY HAVE... ME!
YES, I AM BETROTHED TO YOU
AS THE KING SETTLED BEFOREHAND!
BETWEEN MEN AND WOMEN, THOUGH, THINGS AREN'T THAT EASY.

YOU ARE A SPLENDID KNIGHT.
BUT...YOUR FORTHRIGHT HEART HAS SO LITTLE ROOM FOR LOVE...
WHEN LOVE IS ALL THAT I WANT.
MY ADVANCES LEFT HIM COLD. HE WAS UTTERLY UNMOVED!
HE IS A FINE MONK.

VI SAK HA

DO YOU STILL WANT TO DRAG HIM TO THE KING?
... ...

IF YOU INSIST ON HAVING THEM TRIED BEFORE THE KING,
I WILL SPEAK THE TRUTH!

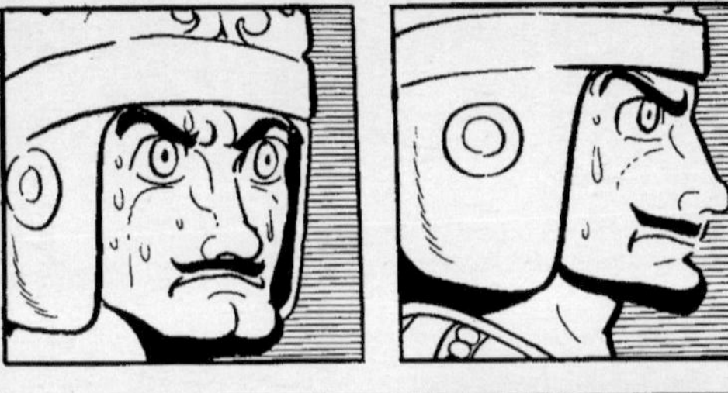

...

A CRIMINAL IS A CRIMINAL. NO MATTER WHAT YOU THREATEN TO TELL HIS MAJESTY, I MUST BY LAW APPREHEND THIS MAN!
THAT IS MY NATURE. ...IF YOU DON'T FIND IT ATTRACTIVE...

I RELEASE YOU FROM OUR PLEDGE.
IT WAS UNLIKE ME TO CLING TO A LOVELESS ENGAGEMENT.

WHAT A DAY. WHAT ELSE HAVE I TO LOSE?
HA... HA HA

CROOKS, I'LL WAIT FOR YOU BELOW.

...

TROOPS !!

THE BANDITS HAVE RUN OFF. THE HOSTAGES AND THE LOOT ARE SAFE.
YOU MAY WITHDRAW! I SHALL CATCH UP WITH YOU. FORM YOUR LINES!

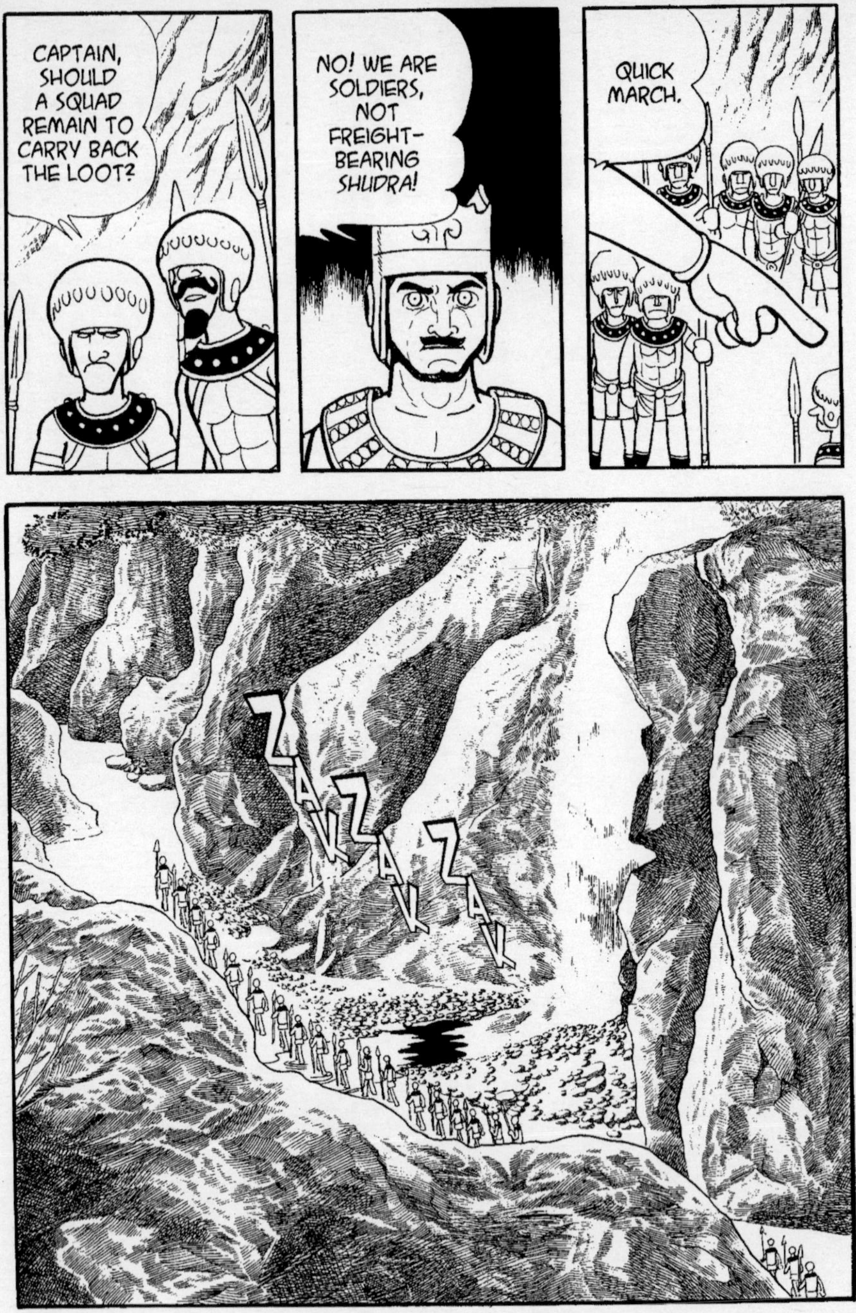

CAPTAIN, SHOULD A SQUAD REMAIN TO CARRY BACK THE LOOT?

NO! WE ARE SOLDIERS, NOT FREIGHT-BEARING SHUDRA!

QUICK MARCH.

ZAK ZAK ZAK

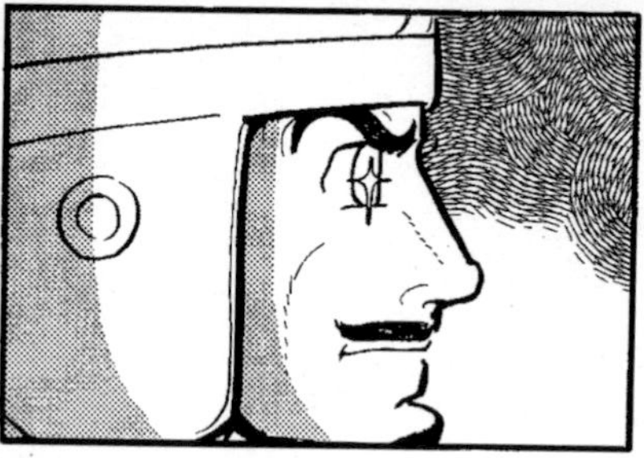

VISAKHA, I'M TERRIBLY SORRY ABOUT ALL OF THIS...
DON'T BE SORRY. YOU'RE NOT TO BLAME, SIDDHARTHA. AND I DON'T BLAME MY FATE, EITHER...

LISTEN UP!

YOU HEARD ALL THAT, RIGHT?
I HAVE TO FULFILL MY PROMISE TO SIDDHARTHA. WE DISBAND AS OF TONIGHT.
WAIT A SEC!
THAT'S PURE WHIMSY, BOSS!

BUT I'M A WHIMSICAL GUY! DIDN'T YA KNOW?
YOU CAN'T JUST DO THIS! THIS IS OUR LIVELIHOOD!
AT LEAST HEAR US OUT!
DISBAND MY ASS
WHERE'S MY PENSION?
WE DEMAND SEVERANCE PAY!!
BACK AT THE DEN,
TAKE ANYTHING OF VALUE. ALL YOU CAN CARRY! THAT'S YER SEVERANCE.
CLAP
CLAP
CLAP
DEAL!
HOORAY
BANZAI CHIEF!
LET'S HAVE A FAREWELL TOAST!
WHAT'S NEXT FOR YOU, BOSS?
ME? I THINK IT'S ABOUT TIME I WENT BACK TO GOOD OL' BEGGING.
SAY, MIGAILA, WOULDJA STILL BE MY LADY OR NO?
OUT OF

I HAVEN'T GOT A CHOICE.

WELL SAI[D] A WIFE'S GOTTA FEEL THAT WAY.

IT'S NOT LIKE THAT, JERK!
WHAT'D I SAY?

YOUR ...
BABY ...

TAKE A LOOK AT MY BELLY, YOU IDIOT!
MIGAILA??

BABY
MY BABY? MIGAILA, YOU... WHY DIDN'T YOU TELL ME ?!
YOU'RE GONNA BE A MOTHER, MIGAILA?

UH

NO FUN BEGGING WITH A BABY TO FEED.
CIAO...
WAIT

DON'T YOU DARE RUN OFF NOW!
I'LL SEND CHILD SUPPORT, I WILL.
YOU IDLE, GOOD-FOR-NOTHING HUSBAND!

YOU'RE STUCK WITH ME FOR LIFE, PAL!!

BOSS, THEM SOLDIERS ARE ALL GONE! NOT A ONE IN SIGHT!
THAT'S WEIRD. THAT DUDE WAS SERIOUSLY HOPING TO CUFF ME, LIKE HE COULD.
SOMETHING'S FUNNY, SIDDHARTHA.
LET'S GO AND SEE.

CHECK THIS OUT! THE KNIGHT'S GONE AND KILLED HIMSELF!

POOR GUY KNEW ONLY ONE WAY TO LIVE...
...

CHAPTER FIVE

INTERVIEW AT MT. PANDAVA

AHOY THERE, MONK.

IN'T THERE NO WATER ROUN' HERE? MY SHEEPS IS NEAR DEAD OF DROUGHT.
NOT ENOUGH FOR A FLOCK. TRY THE YONDER RAVINE, A BROOK MAY RUN IN IT.

I'M DYING OF THIRST MYSELF, OKAY?
BUT THIS IS MY ORDEAL.
MUST BE GREAT TO BE YOU, ASSAJI.

JOLT

SOMEONE JUST PASS?
A SHEPHERD AND HIS FLOCK.

NO! NO! HIS SHEEP IS ALL DIE!
THEY DIE WITH WATER OF POISON!
WHAT DO YOU MEAN?

THERE SOME POOL OF WATER AND THEY DRINK AND GET TUMMY ACHE AND ALL DIE!
DON'T BE RIDICULOUS. HOW CAN YOU KNOW THAT?

HURRY STOP OR ALL DIE.
SNIF

SNIF

A FOOL'S ERRAND! BET THERE'S NO POOL, EVEN.
SNIF
SEE, THERE IS!!

AND SHEEPS. OH, POOR SHEEP ALL DEAD.

THE ROTTING CARCASS OF A TIGER. NO WONDER THE WATER IS DEADLY!
BUT ASSAJI, HOW IN THE WORLD DID YOU KNOW?
SNIF
NOW COME WHIRLWIND.
WHAT?
BIG, BIG WHIRLWINDER COMING.
CUT IT OUT, KID.
YOU'VE BEEN WEIRD EVER SINCE YOU NEARLY DIED OF FEVER.
WE OUGHT TO GO LOOK FOR SIDDHARTHA, WHATEVER HE'S UP TO NOW!
DAMN YOUR WHIRLWIND.
GOTTA RUN. WHIRLWIND COME STRAIGHT FOR US!!
BUT THERE'S NOT A CLOUD IN THE SKY
NOR BREEZE ENOUGH TO STIR A LEAF!
BRODDER, GOTTA RUN!!

WE HIDE IN MOUNTAIN OR WE BLOWN AWAY!
NO GOOD! VILLAGE ALL GONE SOON.
WE'LL REST FOR A MINUTE IN THAT VILLAGE.
ESCA-A-PE!
WHIRLWINDER COMING! THIS VILLAGE, IMPERULD! HURRY RUN TO MOUNTAINS!
ALL YOU RUNNN!!
GA! LOAD OF CRAP!
LIAR
YOU DON'T MEAN TO PILFER THROUGH OUR THINGS WHILE WE'RE IN A PANIC?

YOU DON'T SAY!
IT'S TRUE. THIS BOY SEES INTO THE FUTURE.
I STILL THINK WE'VE BEEN HAD.
WE'LL BE THE BUTT OF JOKES.
HEIGH HO, HEIGH HO!
HOW FAR MUST WE GO?
GO BEHIND MOUNTAIN.
LOOK YE NOW! 'TIS GETTING DARK.
WHOA! LOOK AT THAT!
OH MY!
WOW

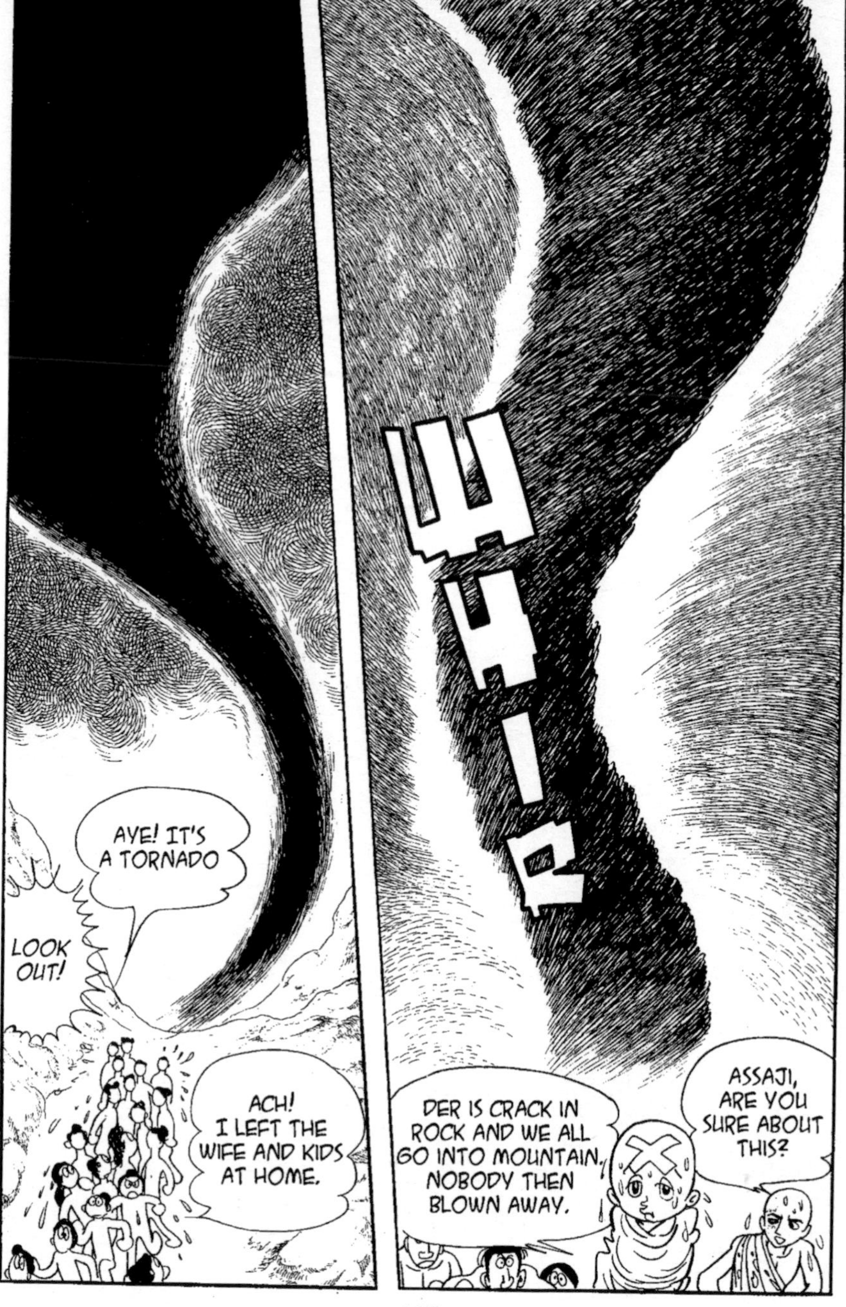
ASSAJI, ARE YOU SURE ABOUT THIS?
DER IS CRACK IN ROCK AND WE ALL GO INTO MOUNTAIN. NOBODY THEN BLOWN AWAY.
AYE! IT'S A TORNADO
LOOK OUT!
ACH! I LEFT THE WIFE AND KIDS AT HOME.

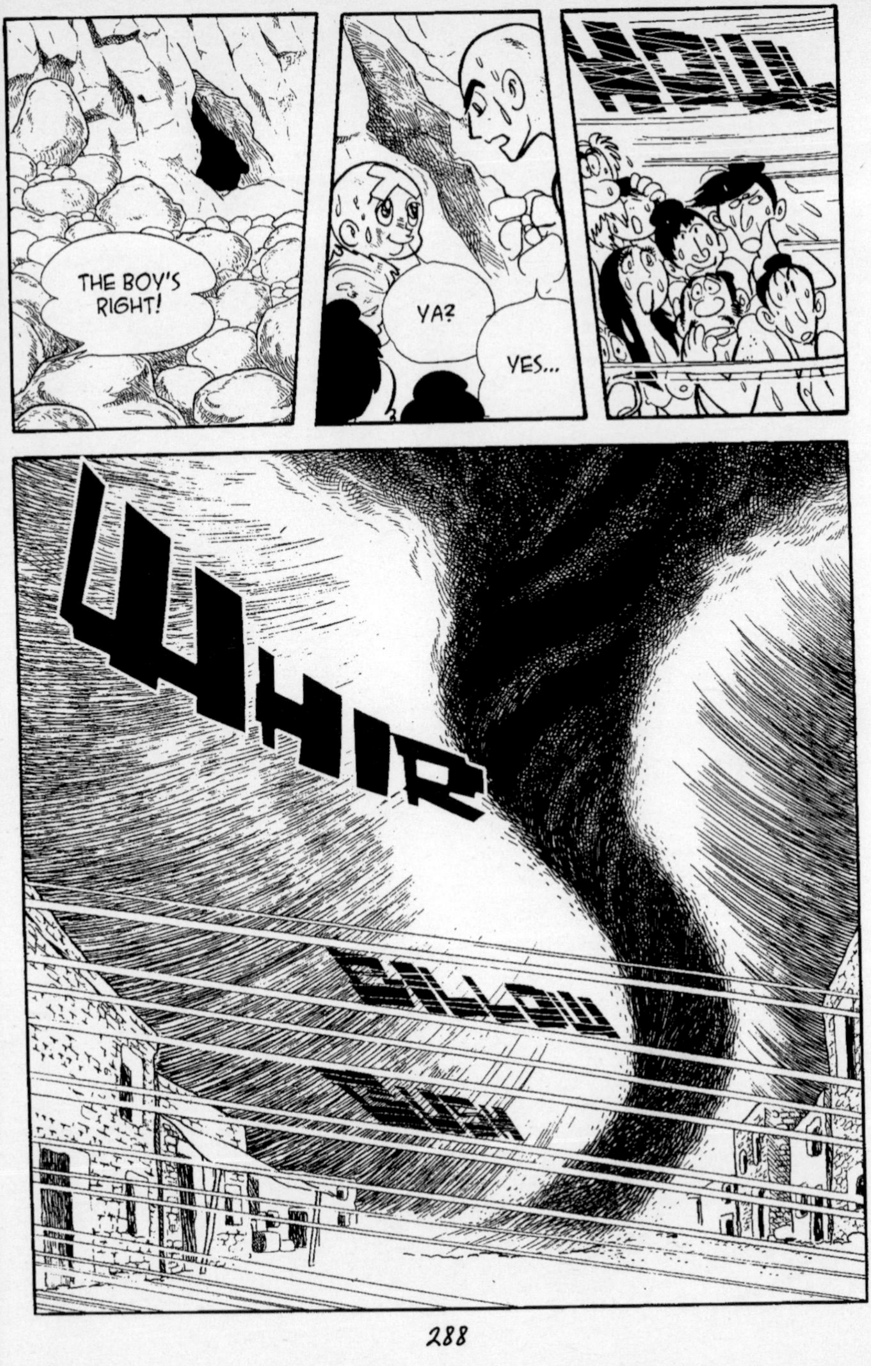

THE BOY'S RIGHT!
YA?
YES...
WHIR

MAGADHA

CLAMOR

CLAMOR

CLAMOR

I HAVE NO USE FOR THE "SPECIAL POWERS" OF SWINDLERS.
MAJESTY, THE BOY IS HERE ALREADY.

THAT SNOT-NOSED BOY IS A PROPHET?

FOR HIS OWN SAKE, I'LL EXPOSE HIS FAKERY AND TEACH HIM A LESSON.
BRING HIM TO ME.

I AM KING BIMBISARA, KING OF ALL MAGADHA. ARE YOU THE PRODIGY WHO SEES INTO THE FUTURE?

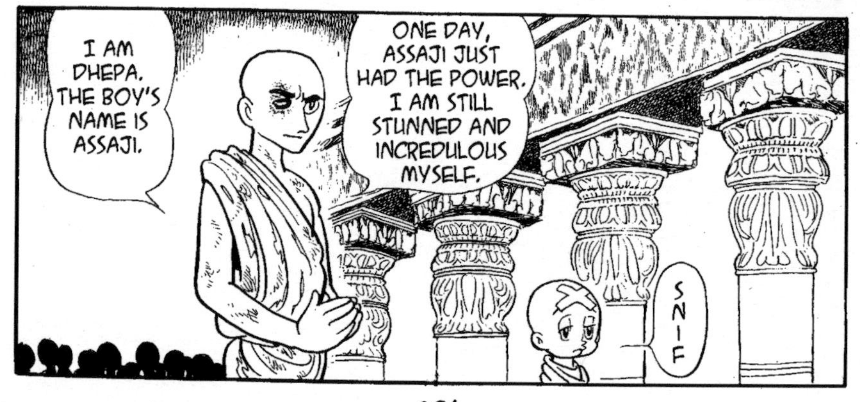

TELL ME, ASSAJI. IS MY FUTURE BLESSED OR CURSED?
KING, YOU GONNA DIE.
DIE KILLED.
NOT SO FAST. HOW SHALL I DIE? FROM ILLNESS?
INSOLENT FRAUD!
SO I AM TO BE KILLED? A GRAVE MATTER. WHO IS THE ASSASSIN?
YOUR SON...
TWENTY YEARS FAR, YOUR SON KILL YOU MAJESHTEE AND HE TOO GET PUNISHED.

VERY WELL. THERE IS A TRAP IN THIS HALL, AND YOU WILL LOSE YOUR LIFE A MINUTE FROM NOW.
UNLESS YOU DIVINE THE TRAP.

IF YOU LIVE, I WILL BELIEVE YOU.
SO TRY AND SAVE YOURSELF, HMM?

THIS IS NO JEST, CHILD!
SNIF

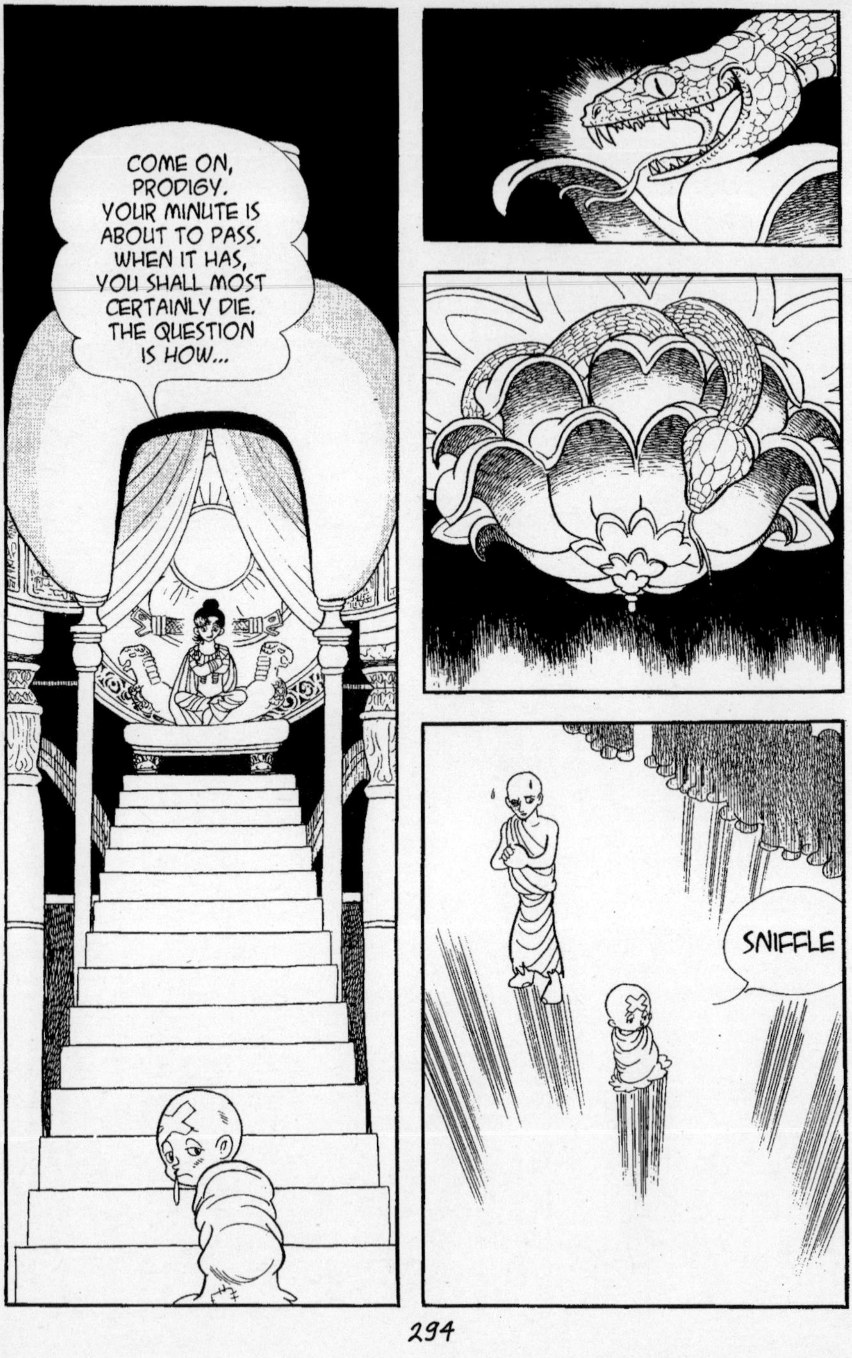

COME ON, PRODIGY. YOUR MINUTE IS ABOUT TO PASS. WHEN IT HAS, YOU SHALL MOST CERTAINLY DIE. THE QUESTION IS HOW...

ASSAJI, I FEAR FOR YOUR LIFE!
IF YOU DON'T HAVE A CLUE, GIVE UP AND APOLOGIZE TO HIS MAJESTY!
TEN SECONDS LEFT.
ONE
TWO
THREE
FOUR!
FIVE!
SIX!
SEVEN!
EIGHT!
NINE!
?
?
?
?
?

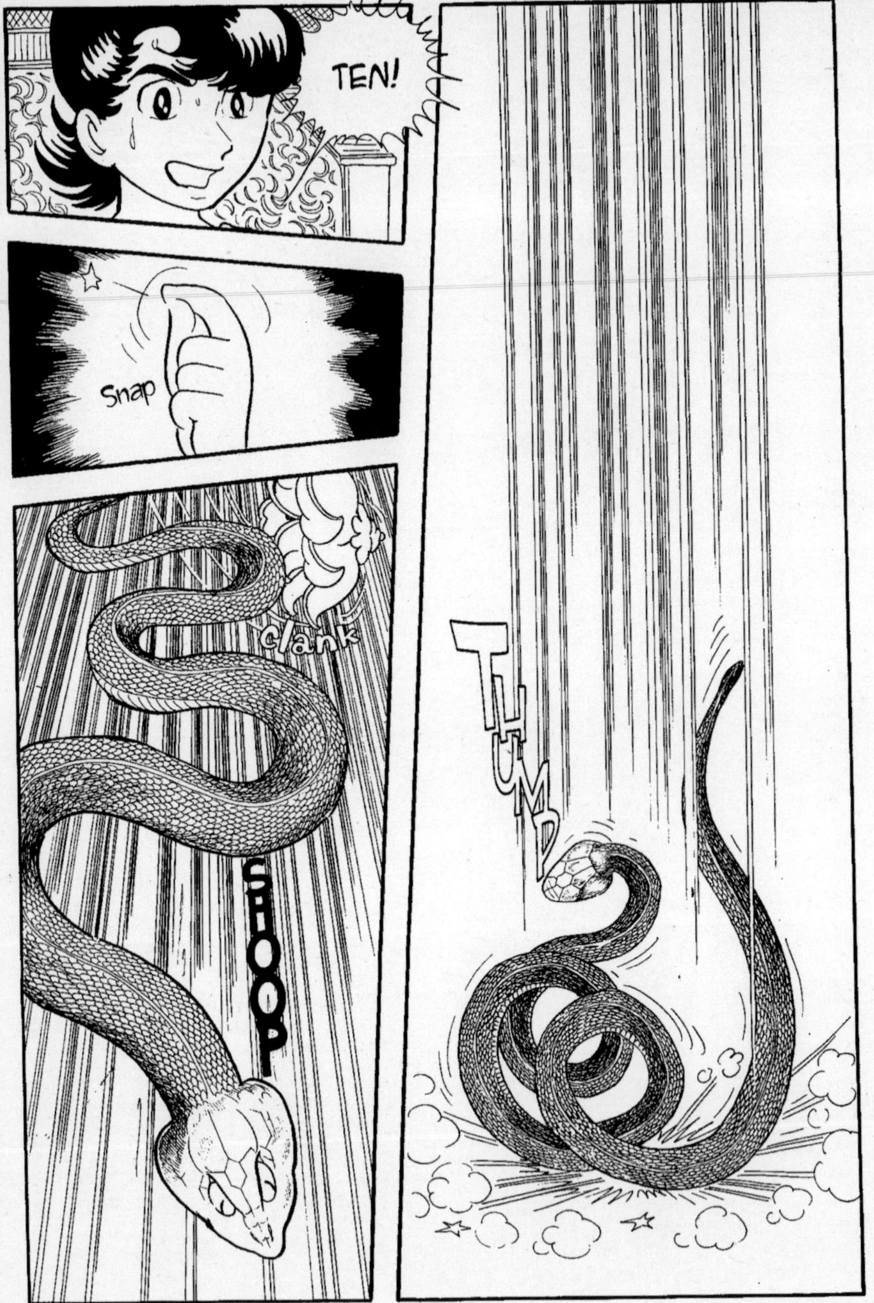
TEN!
Snap
clank
SHOOP
THUMP

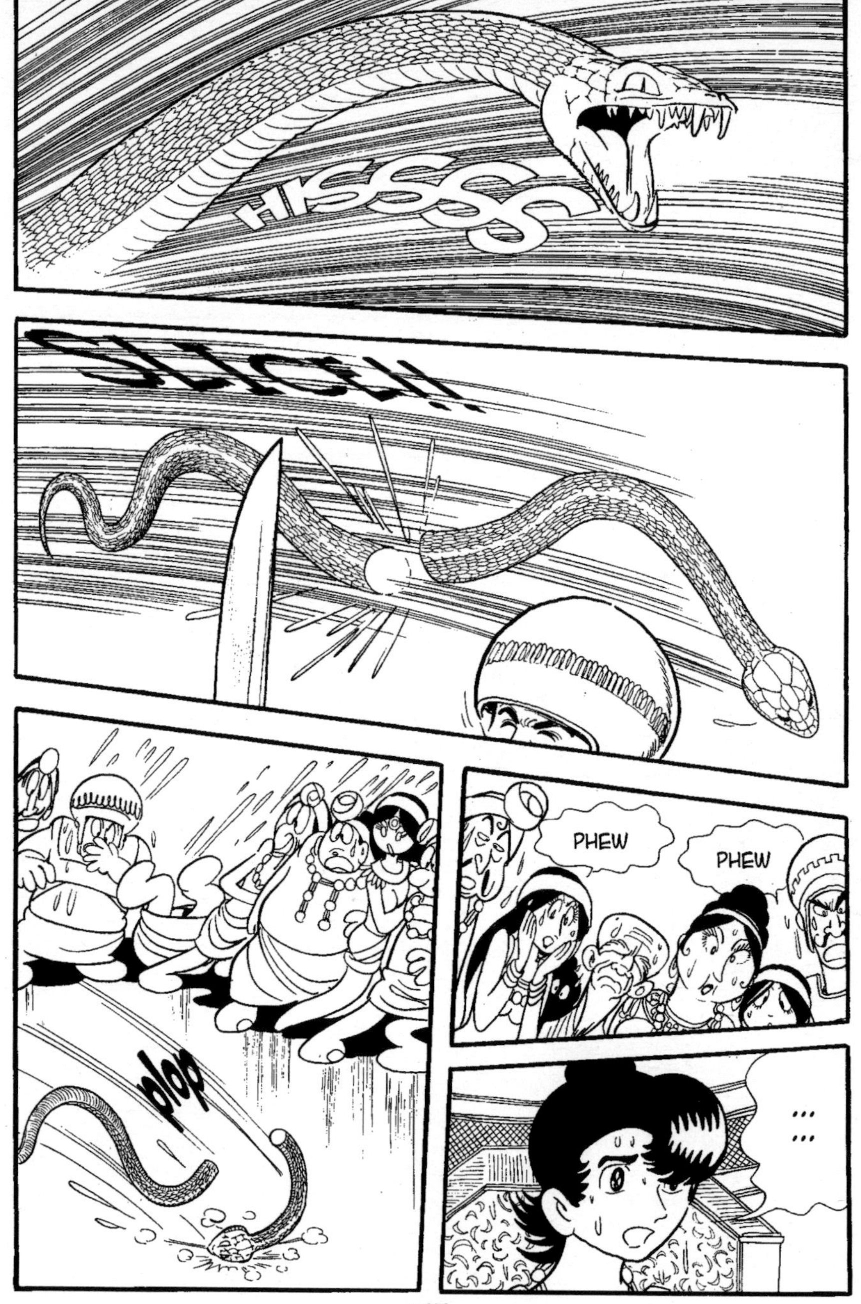
HISSSS
SLICE!!
PHEW
PHEW
plop
...
...

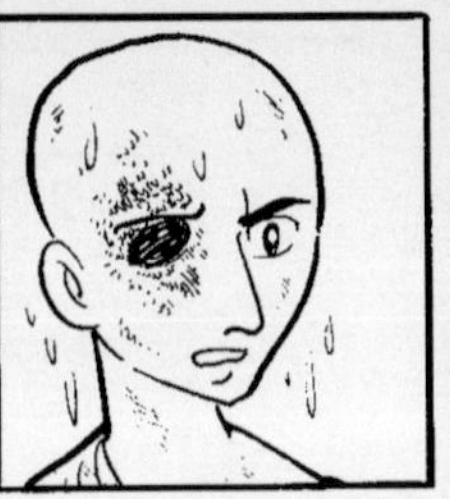

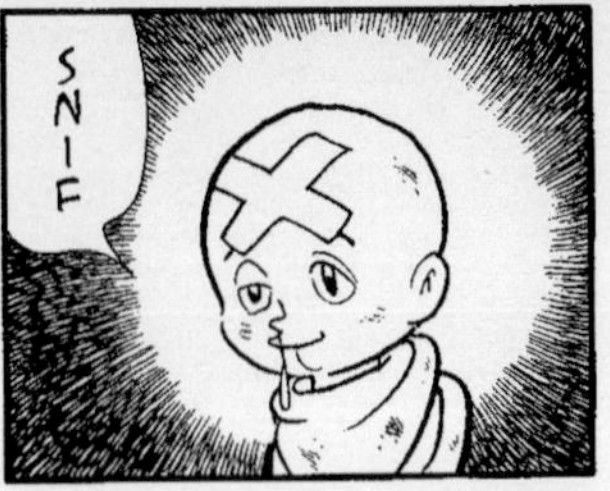

GUESSED THE COURSE THE SNAKE WOULD TAKE,

AND PLACED A SWORD IN ITS PATH. I AM QUITE IMPRESSED.

TWITCH

AND SO, YOUR PROPHECY...

THAT IN TWENTY YEARS I AM TO BE MURDERED BY MY OWN SON...

IS NOT SO EASY TO DISMISS.

LORD, DO NOT BELIEVE HIM!

HE IS JUST A TWO-BIT FORTUNE TELLER!

THROW THE WRETCH IN THE DUNGEON!

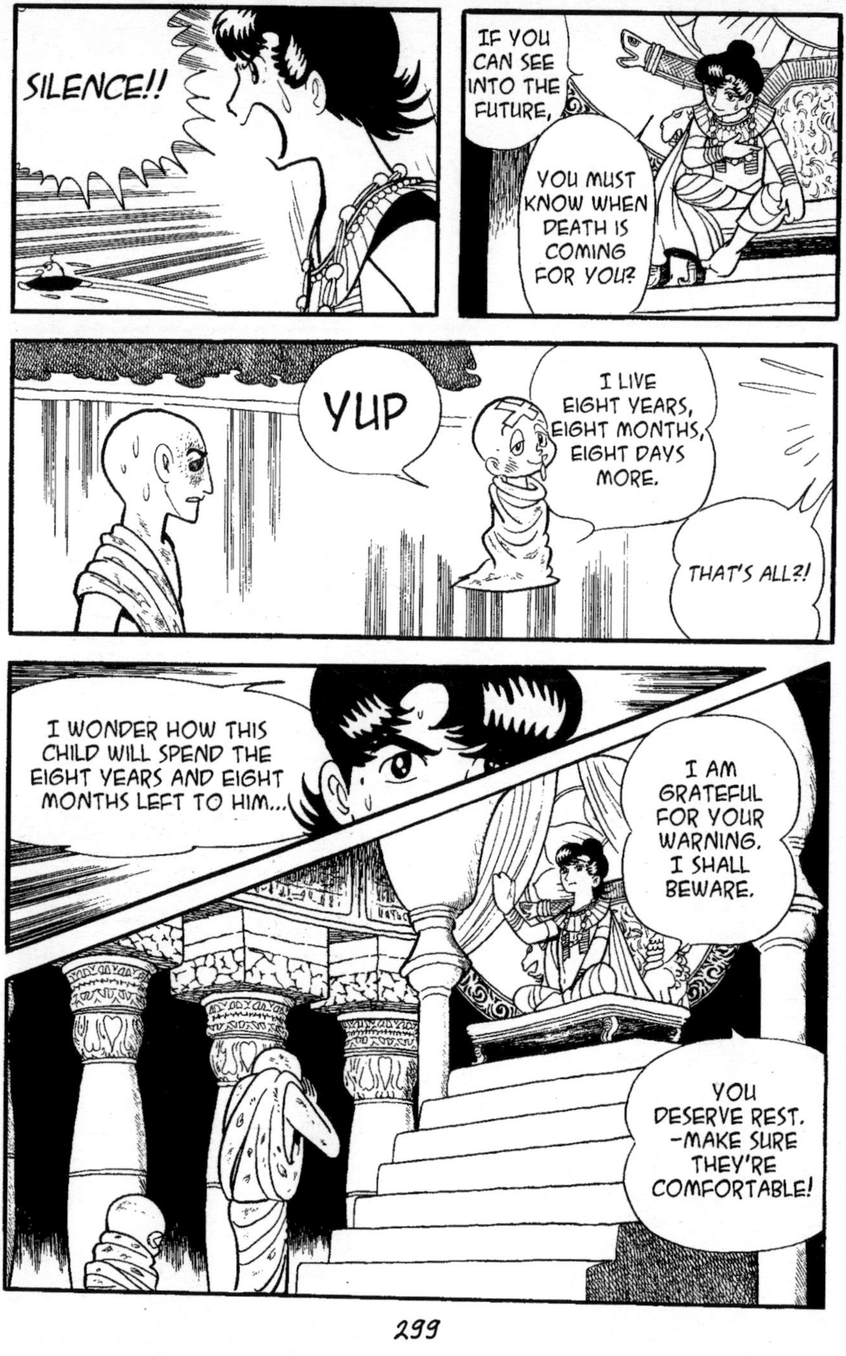

I AM GRATEFUL FOR YOUR WARNING. I SHALL BEWARE.

I WONDER HOW THIS CHILD WILL SPEND THE EIGHT YEARS AND EIGHT MONTHS LEFT TO HIM...

YOU DESERVE REST. -MAKE SURE THEY'RE COMFORTABLE!

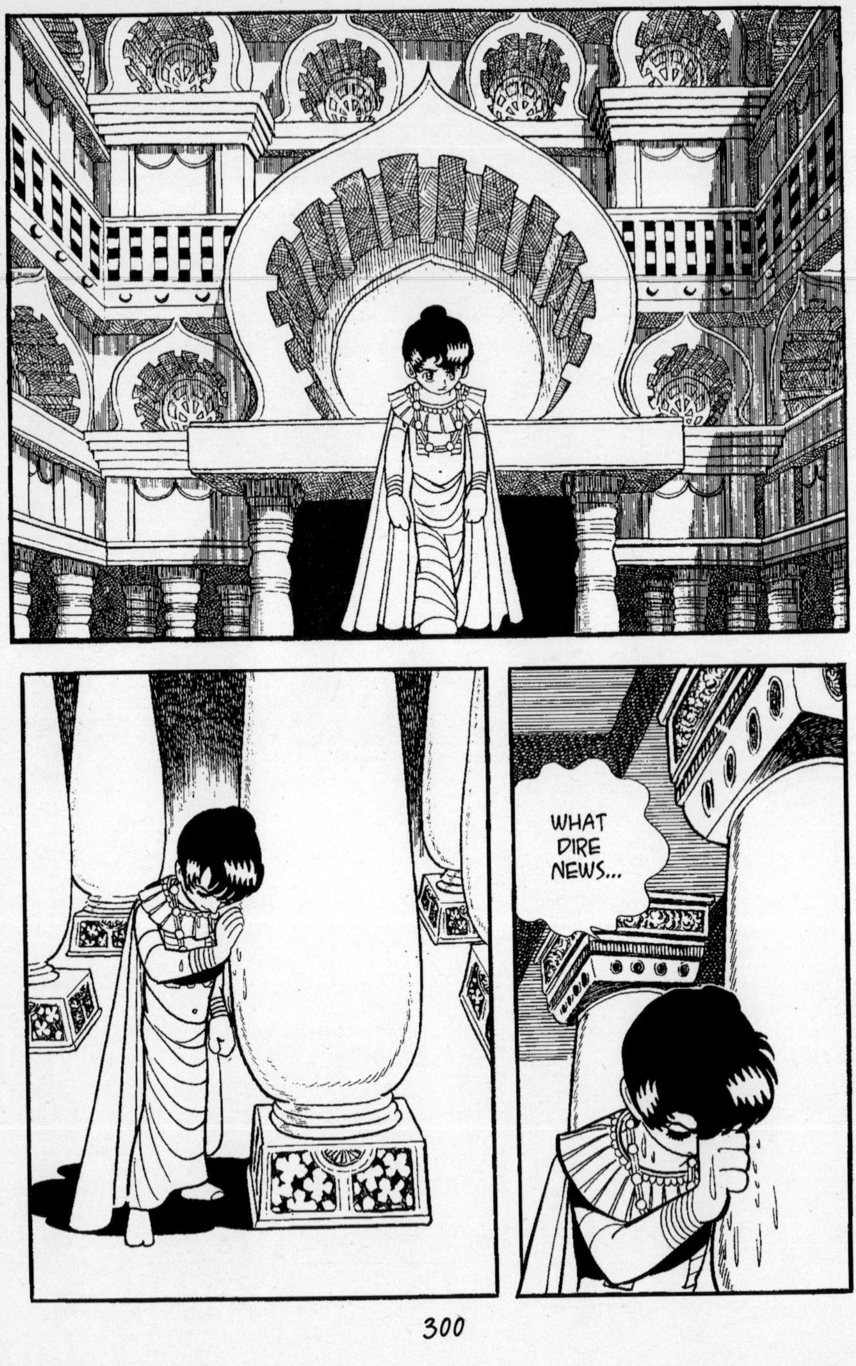

WHAT DIRE NEWS...

MY DESTINY !
MY FUTURE !
I, SLAIN BY MY OWN SON!

I HAVE NOT BEEN AN UNJUST OR INEPT RULER. THE PEOPLE PROSPER, AND THE COUNTRY FLOURISHES. THE KINGDOM OF MAGADHA, THE NEW CENTER OF CULTURE, IS THE ENVY OF ALL ITS NEIGHBORS.

WHY?
WHY SHOULD I BE KILLED BY MY OWN SON? THE CROWN PRINCE?
IS THAT TRULY MY FATE?
MY OWN INESCAPABLE FATE?

THERE ARE THREE WAYS TO PREVENT IT. FIRST: SIRE NO PRINCE.
SECOND: KILL AT BIRTH ANY PRINCE I BEGET.
THIRD: EXILE THE PRINCE TO A DISTANT LAND FROM WHENCE HE CANNOT REACH ME.
BUT PERHAPS ALL SUCH MEASURES ARE FUTILE.
I HAVE ONLY TWENTY YEARS LEFT!
WHAT CAN I ACHIEVE IN TWO MEASLY DECADES?

TELL ME, ASSAJI.
HOW DID YOU GAIN THIS GREAT POWER?

REALLY WANNA KNOW?

VERY MUCH!! TELL ME.

I DIED ONCE.
IN FEVER.
YOU DID ?

YUP. I MET GOD IN DREAM.

AND GOD SAY...
I ONLY LIVE TEN YEARS, SO HE GIMME A POWER.

ARE YOU TELLING ME... YOU'VE BEEN TO THE REALM OF DEATH?

ANYWAY I SEE FUTURE FROM THEN.

...I'M SORRY, THAT'S HARD TO BELIEVE.
YUP, AGREE!

THERE WAS A TIME WHEN I CRAVED THE POWER OF PROPHECY.
BUT I FIGURED THAT SEEING TOO WELL INTO THE FUTURE...
WOULD ROB LIFE OF MEANING.

YOU'RE SO CUTE! PLEASE DO US A FAVOR!
NO, NO, MASTER ASSAJI!
NOSTRADAMUS!

TELL US OUR FUTURES!
YOU KNOW, LIKE, WHO WILL I MARRY? WILL I LIVE LONG?
SNIF

DON'T JUST EAT. PLEASE...

SNIF

SAY, HOW LONG WILL I LIVE?
SNIF
NINEY -TWO

92 YRS OLD ?!
THAT LONG? WONDERFUL!

BUT YOU BE DRIED-UP, GUMMY-EYED, CRANKY CRAZY OLD HAG, DIRTY SACK-OF-BONES.

...
wilt
SNIF

I WANT TO KNOW ABOUT MY FUTURE HUSBAND!
SNIF
YOU MARRY SLEAZY SMUTTY EX-CON SWINDLER.

UM, MY PROSPECTS, IN A NUTSHELL.

DIE IN DITCH.

...
...

IT'S A CRUEL THING TO LEARN YOUR FATE. WHY MUST THEY KNOW?

AH!... I SEE!
I SEE SIDATHA COME!!

REALLY?

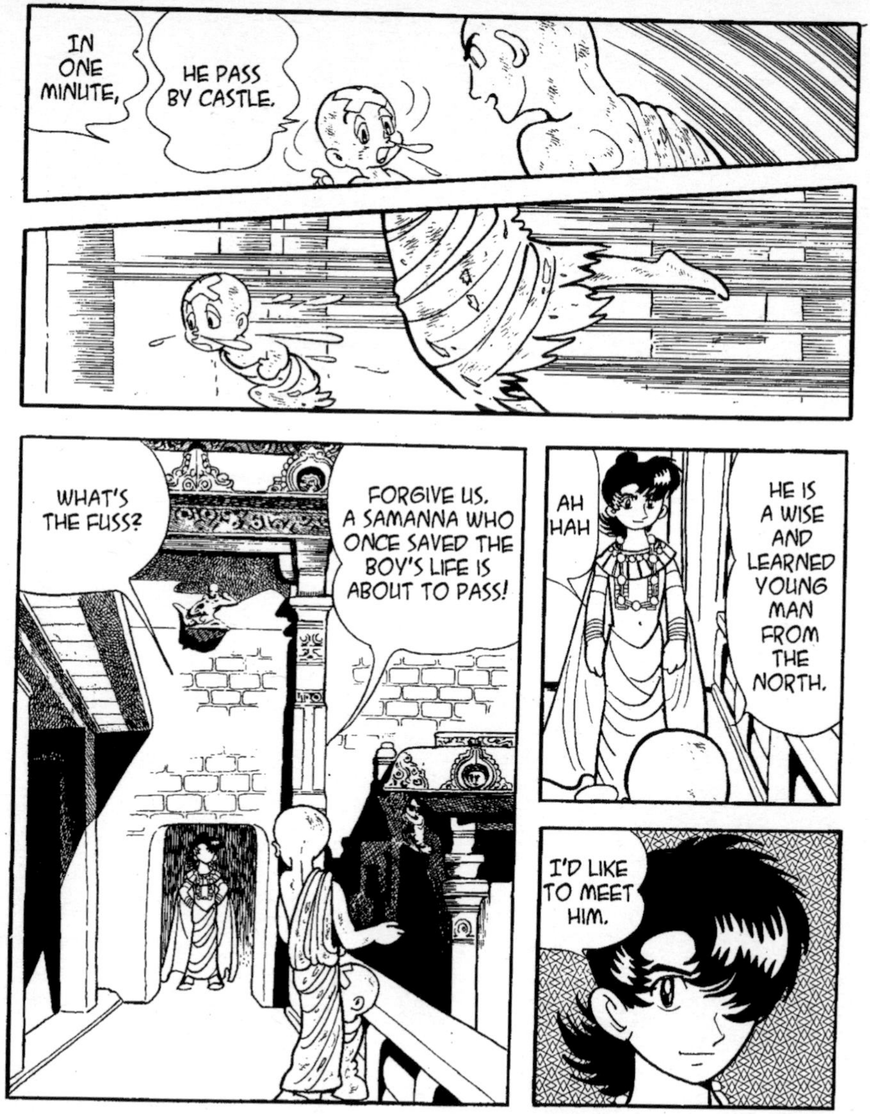

IN ONE MINUTE,
HE PASS BY CASTLE.
WHAT'S THE FUSS?
FORGIVE US. A SAMANNA WHO ONCE SAVED THE BOY'S LIFE IS ABOUT TO PASS!
AH HAH
HE IS A WISE AND LEARNED YOUNG MAN FROM THE NORTH.
I'D LIKE TO MEET HIM.

HUBBUB
HUBBUB

WAHAA! SIDATHA!
SNIF
SIDDHARTHA, UP HERE! IT'S US!
THAT IS NO ORDINARY MENDICANT! PROUD, PURE AND CALM... HE CANNOT BE OF HUMBLE BIRTH!! WHO IS HE?!

FOLLOW THE SAMANNA WHO JUST PASSED! FIND OUT WHERE HE STAYS AND WHERE HE MEANS TO GO!
GUARD!

I CANNOT LET YOU GO NOW.
WAIT, YOU TWO!

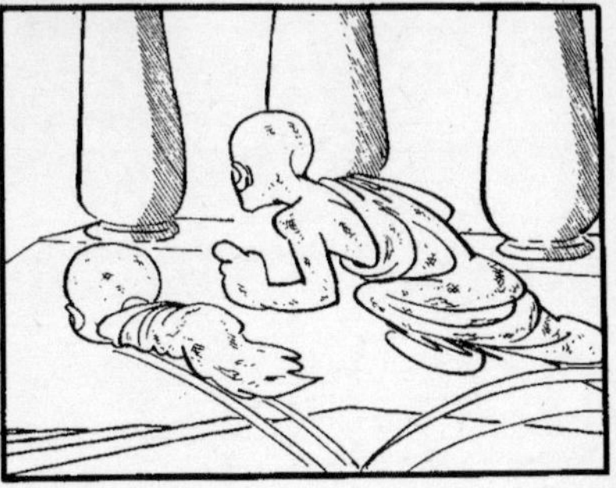

AFTER MY MEN FIND OUT ALL ABOUT HIM, YOU MAY SEE HIM.
WE'VE BEEN LOOKING FOR HIM!

WHY ARE WE FOLLOWING THIS NOVICE ALL OVER THE DAMN CITY?
WANNA BE FIRED? THE KING WISHED IT!

WHAT DID YOU FIND?
YOUR MAJESTY, THE MONK SITS ATOP A BOULDER WAY UP MOUNT PANDAVA.

MOUNT PANDAVA? THAT'S TO THE NORTH OF HERE.

PREPARE A CHARIOT, RIGHT NOW. I WISH TO MEET THIS ASCETIC.
KING, WHY THE HASTE?
IT'S NOT PROPER.
DO AS I SAY! I WILL NOT TOLERATE ANY DISSENT ON THIS MATTER.

STEP
STOMP
STEP

YOUR CHARIOT CAN TRAVEL NO FARTHER.
HE IS UP THIS CLIFF.
THEN I SHALL CLIMB.
MAJESTY, WE WILL READY A PALANQUIN. PLEASE WAIT.
DON'T BOTHER. I CAN WALK.
PLEASE, WAIT!

WHO GOES THERE?! STATE YER BIZNESS!!

I AM THE KING OF MAGADHA, BIMBISARA. I SEEK THE SAMANNA WHO PRACTICES HERE.

K-K-K-KING OF MAGADHA ?!

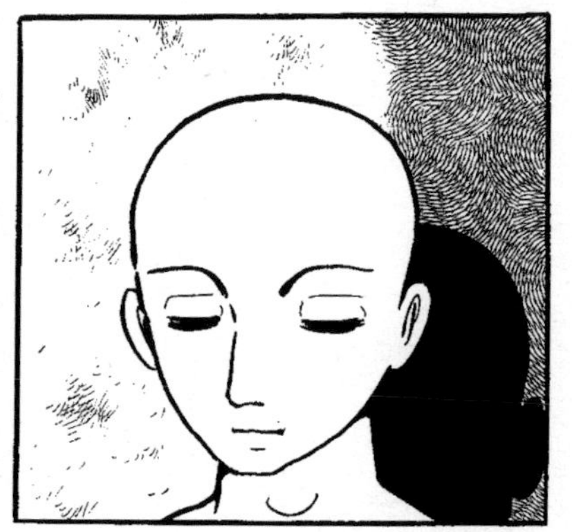

I WAS RIGHT, THIS IS NO ORDINARY MONK.
I'VE ALREADY TAKEN A GREAT LIKING TO HIM.
WELCOME TO MAGADHA, YOUNG SAMANNA.
I AM KING BIMBISARA. IT IS WITH UTMOST JOY THAT I GREET YOU.

KING, FAR NORTH OF HERE, IN THE HIMALAYAS, LIVE A PEOPLE.
THE SHAKYA ARE A WEALTHY, BRAVE, AND RESOURCEFUL TRIBE. I BELONGED TO ITS ROYAL FAMILY UNTIL I RENOUNCED EVERYTHING TO PURSUE THIS LIFE.

YOU ARE YET YOUNG. YOUR LIFE IS JUST ABOUT TO BEGIN!
DO YOU KNOW HOW GALLANT YOU LOOK? YOU EXUDE THE VIRILITY AND GRACE OF A TRUE WARRIOR!
...I BID YOU REMAIN IN MY KINGDOM...

HARKEN TO THE KING'S PLEA.
ALL THE RICHES YOU DESIRE ARE YOURS!
I WILL ENTRUST MY ARMY TO YOU!
AND BECOME A GENERAL OF MYTHIC FAME!

- THESE EYES HAVE SEEN DIVERSE MISFORTUNES FOLLOW FROM DIVERSE DESIRES.

I HAVE CHOSEN TO PUT ALL THAT BEHIND AND TO PURSUE THE ASCETIC'S WAY.
THAT IS MY ONLY SOLACE NOW.

I SEE HOW THAT MAY BE.
BUT... YOU HAVE...

THE FACE OF A KING!
SUCH A WASTE!

...

WILL YOU NOT HEED MY WISHES? I BESEECH YOU.

I WAS AFRAID YOU WOULD REFUSE... ... VERY WELL...
WILL YOU AT LEAST LEND ME YOUR EARS, NOW AND THEN, AS A HOLY MAN?

YOUR MAJESTY HAS WORRIES?
YES! I... DO NOT FEAR DEATH, BUT...
BUT I WISH TO KNOW HOW TO PREPARE FOR IT.

I WOULD GLADLY HOLD CONVERSE WITH YOU.

AH, GOOD !
THIS WAS WORTH THE TRIP.

"BUDDHA" (ENLIGHTENED ONE) !

'TIL WE MEET AGAIN...

TO BE CONTINUED...

BUDDHA
ブッダ
UME 4: THE FOREST OF URUVELA
OSAMU TEZUKA

IN VOLUME 4, SIDDHARTHA SUFFERS ORDEALS IN THE FOREST OF URUVELA. SEATED UNDER THE PIPPALA TREE, HE WILL ACHIEVE ENLIGHTENMENT.

MEANWHILE, KOSALA'S PRINCE VIRUDHAKA LEARNS THAT HIS MOTHER IS OF SLAVE ORIGIN. ENRAGED, HE AND HIS FATHER PRASENAJIT LAUNCH A FINAL WAR AGAINST KAPILAVASTU.

PART THREE (CONTINUED)

CHAPTER SIX

IN THE FOREST OF TRIALS

MIGHTY IS MAGADHA'S REALM
FERTILE FIELDS AND HAMLETS FAIR
RIDGES BLUE AND BUBBLING BROOKS
OUR GLO-RIOUS LORD
LOFTY LIKE THE ELEPHANT AND LIKE THE JACKAL BOLD
LAMB-EYED
SERPENT-FANGED

O JOYOUS DAY THAT HE WAS BORN, O SENIYA BIMBISARA, KING

HAPPY BIRTHDAY
HOORAY!
RAY

SO IT IS MY BIRTHDAY ...
I'VE GAINED ANOTHER YEAR...
IT MEANS THE DAY I MUST DIE HAS COME NEARER.

THOSE CHEERS SOUND TO ME LIKE THE REAPER'S JEERS...

NO MAN KNOWS EXACTLY WHEN HE WILL DIE.

HE GOES ABOUT HIS LIFE, STUDYING, PLAYING, FALLING IN LOVE, WORKING...

AND ONE DAY, LIKE A BLAST OF WIND,
COMES DEATH!

NO ONE KNOWS WHEN IT'S COMING, UNTIL IT DOES.
THAT'S WHY PEOPLE ARE HAPPY AND CAREFREE.
BUT I...
I HAVE LEARNED WHEN AND HOW I SHALL DIE!
IN 19 YEARS, I WILL BE SLAIN.
MUST I ENDURE THIS PAIN UNTIL MY LAST MOMENT?!
YOUR MAJESTY, BUDDHA AND HIS COMPANIONS ARE AT THE PALACE. A BUCK OR TWO IN ALMS SHOULD MOVE THEM ON.
BUDDHA IS HERE?
HEAVENS, BUDDHA!!

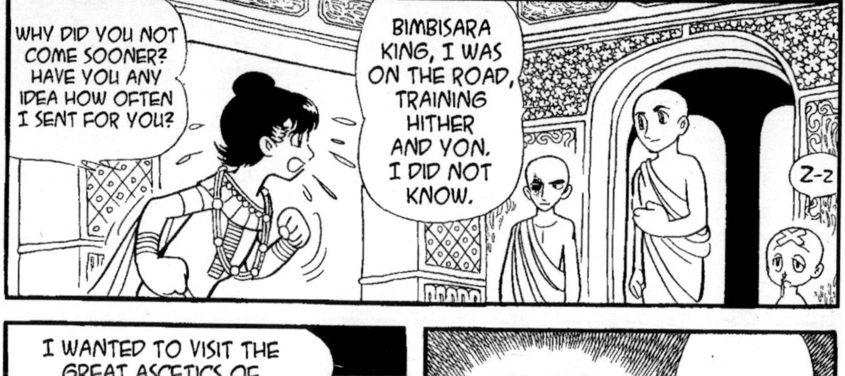

BUDDHA! YOU AND I ARE THE SAME AGE AND HAVE THE SAME BACKGROUND AND THE SAME CONCERNS. DIDN'T YOU PROMISE TO BE MY FRIEND?

INDEED. I DID PROMISE...

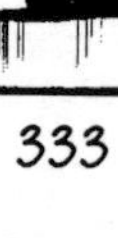